IN HIM

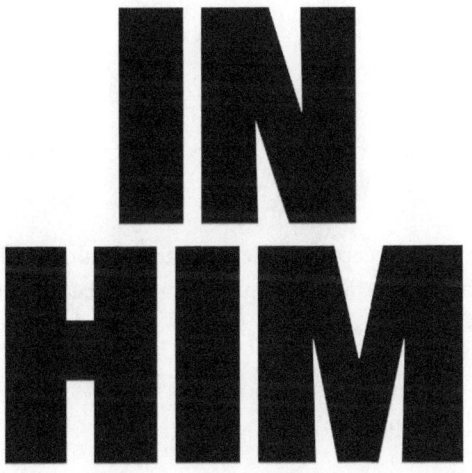

IN HIM

DISCOVERING YOUR IDENTITY IN CHRIST

By: A Monk from St Macarius Monastery

ST SHENOUDA PRESS
SYDNEY, AUSTRALIA
2024

In Him: Discovering you Identity in Christ
By: A Monk from St Macarius Monastery

COPYRIGHT ©2024
St. Shenouda Press

All rights reserved. Except for brief quotations in critical publications or reviews, no part of this book may be reproduced in any manner without prior written permission from the publisher.

ST SHENOUDA PRESS
8419 Putty Rd,
Putty, NSW, 2330
Sydney, Australia

www.stshenoudapress.com

ISBN 13: 978-1-7635450-2-1

All scripture quotations, unless otherwise indicated, are taken from the New King James Version®. Copyright © 1982 by Thomas Nelson, Inc. Used by permission. All rights reserved.

Cover Design:

Mina Rizkalla
www.minarizkalla.com.au

Contents

Chapter 1: An overview of the letter to the Ephesians   7
- The preferred way to study this message   17

Chapter 2: The Opening Anthem   21
- A General Introduction   21
- "In christ": The Key Phrase In The Letter To The Ephesians   25
- The Phrase "In Christ" In Ethical Guidelines   29
- The Phrase "In The Lord" In The Simplest Matters   31

Chapter3: "Blessed Be The God And Father Of Our Lord Jesus Christ..." (Ephesians 1:3)   35
- "The Father Of Our Lord Jesus Christ"   37
- "...The One Who Has Blessed Us With Every Spiritual Blessing..."   40
- "With Every Spritual Blessing"   42
- "With All Spiritual Blessings In The Heavens"   46
- "With Every Spiritual Blessing In The Heavens In Christ"   49
- A Reading From The Book "Faith In Christ" By Our Spiritual Father (Father Matthew The Poor)   50
- Quotes From Saint Athanasius   52
- The Fourth Chapter "He Chose Us In Him Before The Foundation Of The World..."   53

Chapter 4: "Just As He Chose Us In Him Before The Foundation Of The World…" (Ephesians 1:3)   57

-"He Chose Us In Him. To Be Holy And Blameless In Love."   58

-"Before God"   60

-"In Love"   61

-"Adoption Through Jesus Christ Himself"   65

Chapter 5: "To Unite All Things In Christ" (Ephesians 1:10)   69

-The Fundamental Verse In Saint Irenaeus' Theology   69

-The Mystery Of God   73

-The Administration Of The Fulfillment Of The Times   79

-"To Gather Together In One All Things In Christ."   83

-"Which Are In Heaven And Which Are On Earth."   92

-"The Goal Of Incarnation Christ Gathering Everything In Himself"   95

CHAPTER 1

An overview of the Letter to the Ephesians

A reading from Saint Paul[1] the Apostle's Letter to the Ephesians:

"Blessed be the God and Father of our Lord Jesus Christ, who has blessed us with every spiritual blessing in the heavenly places in Christ, just as He chose us in Him before the foundation of the world, that we should be holy and without blame before Him in love, having predestined us to adoption as sons by Jesus Christ to Himself, according to the good pleasure of His will, to the praise of the glory of His grace, by which He made us accepted in the Beloved.

In Him we have redemption through His blood, the forgiveness of sins, according to the riches of His grace which He made to abound toward us in all wisdom and prudence, having made known to us the mystery of His will, according to His good pleasure which He purposed in Himself, that in the dispensation of the fullness of the times He might gather together in one all things in Christ, both which are in heaven and which are on earth—in Him. In Him also we have obtained an inheritance, being predestined according to the purpose of Him who works all things according to the counsel of His will, that we who first trusted in Christ should be to the praise of His glory."[2]

---

[1] Tape number 38 dated October 26, 1989
[2] Ephesians 1: 3-14

In Him you also trusted, after you heard the word of truth, the gospel of your salvation; in whom also, having believed, you were sealed with the Holy Spirit of promise, who is the guarantee of our inheritance until the redemption of the purchased possession, to the praise of His glory."

This book provides a general overview of the Letter to the Ephesians and a tantalising glimpse of its most significant meanings and what sets it apart.

The letter to the Ephesians is considered the pinnacle and crown of Saint Paul's letters. He wrote it towards the end of his life when he was a prisoner in Rome before his martyrdom. It is a radiant letter with an extraordinary spiritual proclamation and a comprehensive vision of God's plan throughout the ages. A plan that began before the foundation of the world (Eph 1: 4) and which will extend infinitely into the blissful eternity until everything is gathered under one head[3], in Christ (Eph 1: 10), until we are filled with all the fullness of God (Eph 3: 19). Saint Paul refers to this plan as "the mystery of Christ."[4] The word "mystery" is repeated many times in this letter[5], and the "mystery of Christ" has several synonyms such as "the purpose of the ages"[6] and "the administration of the fullness of times."[7] This letter provides a comprehensive vision of Christ's great and mighty work throughout the ages. When Paul says that "He chose us in Him before the foundation of the world, that we should be holy..."[8], it is revealed that we were in Christ in the mind of God and loved by Him before we existed, before we were created, and even before God created the world. Before all this, God loved us, because He saw us in Christ and loved our image, which is in the image of Christ. Therefore, the work of

---

[3] The verb "gather" in this verse comes in Greek as ἀνακεφαλαιώσασθαι, in which we notice the same root of the word κεφαλή = head, hence the meaning is: "gather under one head".

[4] μυστήριον τοῦ Χριστοῦ (Ephesians 3:4).

[5] The word "mystery" = μυστήριον is repeated in Ephesians 1:9, and 3:3, 3:4, 3:9, and 5:32, and 6:19.

[6] πρόθεσιν τῶν αἰώνων = "purpose of the ages" appeared in Ephesians 3:11.

[7] οἰκονομία τοῦ πληρώματος τῶν καιρῶν is found in Ephesians 1:9.

[8] Ephesians 1:4

An overview of the Letter to the Ephesians

Christ for us begins in eternity "before the foundation of the world"[9] and extends through the ages without end, "until we all reach unity in the faith and in the knowledge of the Son of God and become mature."[10]

This letter speaks of growing "to the measure of the stature of the fullness of Christ"[11], and even being "filled with all the fullness of God"[12]. Note, he says, "with all...", not "by all the fullness of God". This fulfillment is open-ended, limitless, never fully exhausted, but continually growing without end.

This is Apostle Paul's illuminating vision in his grand letter to the Ephesians, which is more comprehensive than his other letters. For example, if we compare it to his letters to the Romans and Galatians, which talk about justification, forgiveness of sins, and free salvation through faith in Christ, we find that in this letter, Saint Paul revisits this topic but embeds it in a more in depth vision. As in the preceding letters, he states: "In Him we have redemption through His blood, the forgiveness of sins"[13] and, " For by grace you have been saved through faith, and that not of yourselves; it is the gift of God, not of works, lest anyone should boast."[14] Here, the apostle revisits the core theme found in Romans and Galatians, namely free salvation and redemption through Christ's blood, but with a brighter and more inclusive vision of Christ's complete work throughout the ages. For instance, after saying that "in Him we have redemption through His blood"[15], he demonstrated that this redemption leads to a plan that for the "fullness of the times He might gather together in one all things in Christ, both which are in heaven and which are on earth—in Him."[16] Christ's work of salvation doesn't stop at forgiveness of sins

---

9 Ibid
10 Ephesians 4:13
11 Ibid.
12 Ephesians 3:19
13 Ephesians 1:7
14 Ephesians 2:8-9
15 Ephesians 1:7
16 Ephesians 1:10

and justification, but extends to gathering everything in Christ. Ultimately, all creation, those "which are in heaven and which are on earth"[17], will come together under one head, in Christ.

In truth, this is "the unsearchable riches of Christ" [18], which far exceeds the issues of justification and salvation from sin and does not stop until all of us are led to the full unity in God and in Christ. " Till we all come to the unity of the faith and of the knowledge of the Son of God, to a perfect man, to the measure of the stature of the fullness of Christ"[19] This is Apostle Paul's vision, as expansive as the "fullness of Christ"[20].

At the end of the first chapter, Paul talks about the church being "His body, the fullness of Him who fills all in all"[21]. Then, in the fourth chapter, he says that Christ "ascended far above all the heavens in order to fill everything"[22]. Here, Paul explains that the purpose of Christ's ascension is to fill everything. He includes us in His fullness, allowing us to be filled "with all the fullness of God"[23].

"The mystery of Christ"[24] (μυστήριον τοῦ Χριστοῦ)- This phrase in the third chapter is the pulsating heart of the entire letter. In fact, when we read this letter, we can perceive the profound "insight" of Apostle Paul into the mystery of Christ, as he himself states. The entire letter revolves around this "mystery". From the first chapter, he talks about the "mystery of His will"[25], then he reveals the content of this mystery is to "gather together in one all things in Christ,"[26]. And in the third chapter, he says that the content of the mystery of Christ is that

---

17 Ibid.
18 Ephesians 3:8
19 Ephesians 4:13
20 Ibid.
21 Ephesians 1:23
22 Ephesians 4:10 NKJV, the verb "fill" in Greek πληρόω and the word "fullness" πλήρωμα are repeated often in the letter to the Ephesians (Eph 1:10 and 23 twice, 3:19 twice, 4:10 and 13, and 5:18), characterizing this letter.
23 Ephesians 3:19
24 Ephesians 3:4
25 Ephesians 1:9
26 Ephesians 1:10

An overview of the Letter to the Ephesians

"the Gentiles should be fellow heirs, of the same body, and partakers of His promise"[27].

Note that the Arabic translation does not highlight the meaning of partnership in each of these three items separately, as is the case in Greek. In the Greek text, it says that the nations are coheirs (sugklhronÒma), co-bodies (sÚsswma), and co-partakers (summštoca) with the prefix συν- (= with or partner) repeating each time. However, the Beirut translation simply uses the word "partners" once, thus diminishing the emphasis on partnership. The original text insists that partnership is in each item of the three items separately.

"Co-bodies" (σύσσωμα) – This is the greatest mystery of Christ. Christ managed to secretly attract all of humanity into His one body. All nations have become (or at least are invited to become) "co-bodies". Christ's work is primarily a gathering one, a work that leads to the gathering of all existence in Himself, in heaven and on earth, according to the definition of "the mystery of His will" that we read in the first chapter, to "gather together in one all things in Christ, both which are in heaven and which are on earth—in Him."[28] The entire universe, all of created existence, is invited to gather under one head in Christ. More than that, all existence absolutely, divine and created existence, gathers in Christ, as it says in the second chapter: "that He might reconcile them both to God in one body through the cross"[29]. The two are the Jews and the Gentiles, who were part of the world in that era. Apostle Paul says that Christ has reconciled these two and brought them together in His blessed person. This is the mystery of Christ who gathers all humanity with God in Himself, as Paul reveals.

But note that this comprehensive vision of Christ's gathering work was not one of Paul's innovations or inventions. Instead, it matches the Lord's own words, whether in the three Synoptic Gospels or in the Gospel according to St. John.

---

27 Ephesians 3:6
28 Ephesians 1:10
29 Ephesians 2:16

IN HIM

In the three Synoptic Gospels, Christ addresses Jerusalem (where Jerusalem represents humanity called to union with God): "O Jerusalem, Jerusalem.. How often I wanted to gather your children together, as a hen gathers her chicks under her wings"[30]. The Lord's choice of the image of a hen gathering her little chicks under her wings is very precise and successful. There is no example in all of creation that vividly illustrates Christ's gathering work like a hen spreading her wings to embrace her chicks, making them into one entity as if they were a single living being. This is an image of utmost creativity and congruence with Christ's work.

As for the Gospel of John, it is undoubtedly the Gospel closest to the spirit of the letter to the Ephesians [31]. If the Gospel of John is characterised by its illuminating vision and high spiritual maturity, John could write this because those he wrote to were at this same level of spiritual maturity that John wrote his Gospel with. This indicates that the ecclesiastical environment in which St. John lived in Ephesus was highly advanced spiritually. Therefore, it's not surprising that St. Paul addresses them in the first line of his letter: "Paul, an apostle of Jesus Christ by the will of God, To the saints who are in Ephesus"[32].

We can imagine that the bishops, priests, and people of Asia Minor (with Ephesus as their capital), who believed through the teachings of the Apostle Paul, would eagerly turn to Saint John when he came to stay with them. They clung to him, persistently asking him, as someone who had lived closely with Jesus and was close to His heart, if what they had heard from Paul was

---

30 Matthew 23:37 and Luke 13:34
31 It is well known that St. John wrote his gospel while living in the city of Ephesus, responding to the urging of the people and leaders of this church. Our spiritual father (Father Matta El Meskeen) in his book "Introduction to the Explanation of St. John's Gospel," says: The letter to the Ephesians reveals the theological level not only reached by St. Paul, but also by those to whom the letter was written,... From this, we understand why this theological depth was earnestly deposited by St. John, inspired by the Spirit, in his gospel for this people! As it is governed by the proportion of 'like for like' (p18).
32 Ephesians 1:1

An overview of the Letter to the Ephesians

based on Jesus' teachings. Or were they just speculations by Paul, with no true foundation in Jesus' words?

Because of this, John wrote his gospel in response to their pressing questions, validating the words of the Apostle Paul. As if he was saying to them: Yes, what Paul said is true. If he told you that the ultimate purpose of Christ's work is to "gather together in one all things in Christ"[33], then indeed the Lord has died to "gather together in one the children of God who were scattered abroad."[34] The scattered children of God are the Jews and the Gentiles, and Christ has come to bring them together, which is the same issue faced between believers of Jewish and Gentile origins, which Paul addressed by saying that Christ "is our peace, who has made both one"[35]. He explains this in great detail until the end of the second chapter. So, John confirmed and validated the words of the Apostle Paul, and told them about the Lord's words: " And other sheep I have which are not of this fold; them also I must bring, and they will hear My voice; and there will be one flock and one shepherd."[36] Who are the other sheep that are not from the fold of Israel but the Gentiles, as the Apostle Paul clarified that they have an essential share in the "mystery of Christ," the content of which is "that the Gentiles should be fellow heirs, of the same body, and partakers of His promise in Christ through the gospel" [37].

Then the people of Ephesus ask Saint John, "Is it true that we are to obtain the glory of our Lord Jesus Christ[38] or is this an exaggeration from the Apostle Paul? Did the Lord say anything about this?" John responds, "Yes, it is true, and I heard the Lord Himself saying in His prayer to the Father that He has given us the glory that the Father gave Him."[39] They then ask him, "But what about our unity with Christ? Is it true that we

---
33 Ephesians 1:10
34 John 11:52
35 Ephesians 2:14
36 John 10:16
37 Ephesians 3:6
38 2 Thessalonians 2:14
39 John 17:24

all become "in Christ" and Christ becomes in us? Did Christ say such a thing, or is this some kind of mysticism invented by Paul?" John answers them and records what he heard from the Lord during His farewell discourse on Maundy Thursday, "At that day you will know that I am in My Father, and you in Me, and I in you... If anyone loves Me, he will keep My word; and My Father will love him, and We will come to him and make Our home with him." [40]

He also tells them what he heard from the Lord during His final prayer, "that they all may be one, as You, Father, are in Me, and I in You; that they also may be one in Us... I in them, and You in Me; that they may be made perfect in one, and that the world may know that You have sent Me, and have loved them as You have loved Me.[41] Therefore, there is a complete agreement between the letters of Paul and the spirit of John's Gospel.

Another point that illustrates the importance of the Ephesians' letter is that it gives us a bright, joyous, and soul-stirring vision of our existence's origin and the purpose to which human existence is headed. It precisely shows us where we came from, where we are going, why we are created, and how we were loved by God before we were even created. All this elevates us and provides us with a stable spiritual anchor, with nothing able to shake us, no matter what.

In mechanics, there's something called stable equilibrium and unstable equilibrium. If you take a rod and hang it from a joint above, this is called stable equilibrium. No matter how much you move it left or right, it will follow your movements but will always return to its vertical position and stable balance. But if you take the same rod and fix it from below (like standing a pen vertically on a desk or attaching a rod to a hinge at its bottom), it may stand upright for a while, but its equilibrium is unstable. With any movement or touch, it will fall and never reach a state of stability. Why? Because its point of balance is <u>below, not above</u>.

---

40 John 14:20,23
41 John 17:21,23

An overview of the Letter to the Ephesians

In reality, if we were suspended from above, if we had this high vision that the saints call "looking above"[42], nothing would be able to shake us or cause us to lose our peace and spiritual stability. Saint Anthony says about this "true gaze" that "there is nothing greater than it in Christian faith, and those who attain it will no longer feel tired in anything, nor will they be distressed out of fear, but the joy of our Lord will comfort them day and night, and the deeds of God will always be sweet to them at all times, and for this, God gives them revelations of the great secrets of the coming age, which we cannot describe with the fleshly tongue"[43].

Because of this, Saint Anthony encourages us to acquire this spiritual gaze, which is the discernment. This is what the Lord said: "The lamp of the body is the eye. If therefore your eye is good, your whole body will be full of light."[44]. That is, if your spiritual vision is healthy, your entire spiritual life will be illuminated.

Thus, our entire life would be lit if we acquire this spiritual vision and this illuminating vision of the work of Christ. If we realise where we came from and where we are going, if we are conscious of our heavenly calling, and what the end of the life we live is, and that we are not created for the earth, we are not created ever for thirty or sixty or eighty years that we spend on earth and then return to the dust of the earth once again. We are created for heavenly glories that have no limit and no end. If our heart is attached from above to these glories, and if this illuminating vision of our spiritual future in Christ is revealed to us; we will be hanging from above like this rod that reached a state of stable equilibrium. Any experience that comes to shake us, even if it moves us right or left, in the end, we will stabilize and return to our fixed vertical position and there will be nothing powerful enough to overcome us, as long

---

[42] St. Amounas, a disciple of St. Anthony, refers to it in his fourth letter, where he repeats the phrase "the transcendent gaze" four times. As for St. Anthony, he refers to it in his eleventh letter as "the true gaze that is discernment."
[43] St Anthonys eleventh letter: 1
[44] Matthew 6:22

IN HIM

as our heart is hung from above: "For where your treasure is, there your heart will be also"[45].

Another fundamental characteristic that the letter to the Ephesians has, is its very high ecclesiastical spirit. From the outset of the letter in the first chapter, it clarifies that the eternal Father's pleasure and the administration of the fullness of times are to "gather together in one all things in Christ, both which are in heaven and which are on earth—in Him." (1:10), where this gathering under one head in Christ is the essence of the church's entity. The first chapter ends with the church as well "which is His body, the fullness of Him who fills all in all" (1:23). In the second chapter, he talks about the unifying work of Christ: "For He Himself is our peace, who has made both one… reconcile them both to God in one body"[46].

Indeed, this body in which the two unite with God is also an expression of the essence of the Church. Also, in the second chapter, he speaks about the single temple built "in Christ": "in whom the whole building, being fitted together, grows into a holy temple in the Lord, in whom you also are being built together for a dwelling place of God in the Spirit.[47]" All of these are Apostle Paul's vision of the Church, which represents the unity of humanity in God. Similarly, in chapters 3, 4, and 5, there are high-level discussions about the Church.

In fact, this letter, with its high ecclesiastical spirit, is the best cure for the most widespread disease in our current era on the church level, which is the disease of fragmentation and division. This is not only at the level of different churches, but even within a single church. Even within one monastery, you find the spirit of factionalism. Everyone lacks the "unity of heart that comes from love", whether at the level of the Church, the monastery, or the family. Therefore, the most healing balm for the wounded body of Christ in our present age is this letter to the Ephesians, whose spirit we must imbibe. The Church invites us every day in the morning prayer to repeat a piece

---

45 Luke 12:34
46 Ephesians 2:14,16
47 Ephesians 4:1-4

An overview of the Letter to the Ephesians

from this letter:

"I, therefore, the prisoner of the Lord, beseech you to walk worthy of the calling with which you were called, with all lowliness and gentleness, with longsuffering, bearing with one another in love, endeavouring to keep the unity of the Spirit in the bond of peace. There is one body and one Spirit, just as you were called in one hope of your calling"[48].

It is noted in this piece that it begins and ends with a repeated mention of the calling to which we were called. So, what is this calling that deserves such attention? It is the purpose for which we were created: to become all "in Christ", to "gather under one head in Christ" (1: 10), to reconcile "in one body with God" (2:16), to be all "partners in the body" (3: 6). Based on this shared calling, he implores us to preserve the unity of the Spirit, and even to be "hastening to keep the unity of the Spirit". So, what does this haste mean? It means that as soon as you feel that this unity with your brother has been injured, you must hasten to him to restore the affinity between you, because he is a member of the body of Christ, he and I are members of the one body of the Lord; so how can I live while causing a fracture in the body of the Lord?

THE PREFERRED WAY TO STUDY THIS MESSAGE

This method has been passed down to all of us from our father Matthew the poor. It is a method once practiced by the early desert fathers throughout the day in their caves. Anyone who was honest and patient and persevered in practicing it, has reaped from the Gospel treasures of great value. This method is, in short: murmuring or repetition, word by word repetition of the Gospel.

Take the first verse and repeat the first word from the first verse, say it over and over again, say it with a raised heart, say it with contemplation, do not leave it until you feel the spiritual depth

---

48 Ephesians 4:1-4

and the spiritual content the word carries. For example, "Blessed be the God and Father of our Lord Jesus Christ. [49]" Take the word: Blessed, repeat it often, blessed, blessed, blessed, pray with it and address God with it. Feel the spiritual magnitude of this meaning and how God is blessed in all His creations, and deserves every blessing, blessed through the ages, blessed in the whole creation. And when you exhaust all you can extract from this meaning, move on to the second word, which is: God, blessed God, say it with reverence, feel the immense content this word carries, what is God? And what is His magnitude? Understand the word with your heart and not with your mind. Then after that, say the two words together, i.e. blessed God, once you repeat them a lot, you will find a new taste and new emotions. And after that, move to the third word of the first verse: the Father, blessed God the Father, feel the meaning of the Father, and ask God as you say it to reveal to you the depths of His fatherhood and its infinite size... Then go back and repeat these three words together: blessed God the Father. And when you get saturated and comprehend; a completely new meaning will be revealed to you that will make you very happy. And then move on to the rest of the verse: blessed be God the Father of our Lord Jesus Christ, that is, God is the Father of Jesus Christ, do not get tired of repeating it, savor it inside your heart.

In truth, everyone who practiced this method and was devoted to it, has gained a lot from it. It's true that it requires effort, patience, and perseverance, and that the result does not appear initially, but like the result of someone who takes an axe and plows the earth, they might tire initially, but in the end, they reap a fruit sweeter than honey.

This practice is what the desert monks did throughout the day in their caves. It was called murmuring (Hazez)[50] by them and in Greek it's μελέτη. This word is common in the Septuagint and corresponds to the Hebrew verb "hagah," which translates

---

49 Ephesians 1:3
50 Refer to the book "Life of Orthodox Prayer", the first chapter, second section: Degrees of Prayer - First: Meditation (Melétē).

An overview of the Letter to the Ephesians

to "murmur" in Arabic: "Blessed is the man who walks not in the counsel of the wicked... but his delight is in the law of the Lord, and on his law, he meditates (meletései) day and night"[51] , meaning to repeat, to murmur, to recite the words in a low voice until they penetrate deeply, and he grasps their hidden spiritual value.

Apply this method in your study of the Gospel, to take each word and absorb the hidden spiritual content in it. Murmuring the words of the Gospel gives you spiritual health, strengthens your bones, establishes your spiritual build, and introduces the word to the depths of your soul "even to the division of soul and spirit, and of joints and marrow" [52]. So, if you then resort to books of explanation and interpretation, you will benefit from them, because the words will have something to correspond with inside you. But if you just read books of explanation and interpretation, without having previously studied the word in a personal study, they will not benefit you much, because the words will find no foundation inside you.

---

51 Psalms 1:1,2
52 Hebrews 4:12

CHAPTER 2

The Opening Anthem

A GENERAL INTRODUCTION

Blessed be the God and Father of our Lord Jesus Christ[1], who has blessed us with every spiritual blessing in the heavenly places in Christ, just as He chose us in Him before the foundation of the world, that we should be holy and without blame before Him in love, having predestined us to adoption as sons by Jesus Christ to Himself, according to the good pleasure of His will, to the praise of the glory of His grace, by which He made us accepted in the Beloved.

In Him we have redemption through His blood, the forgiveness of sins, according to the riches of His grace which He made to abound toward us in all wisdom and prudence, having made known to us the mystery of His will, according to His good pleasure which He purposed in Himself, that in the dispensation of the fullness of the times He might gather together in one all things in Christ, both which are in heaven and which are on earth—in Him. In Him also we have obtained an inheritance, being predestined according to the purpose of Him who works all things according to the counsel of His will, that we who first trusted in Christ should be to the praise of His glory.

In Him you also trusted, after you heard the word of truth, the gospel of your salvation; in whom also, having believed,

---

[1] Tape number 39 dated November 2, 1989

you were sealed with the Holy Spirit of promise, who is the guarantee of our inheritance until the redemption of the purchased possession, to the praise of His glory. This piece is considered a spiritual anthem at the highest level, praising God for the spiritual blessings He has given us in Christ. The whole anthem is one continuous paragraph; you won't find a single spot where you can pause, from the first: "Blessed be God..." to the end of verse 14: "...to the praise of His glory." It's all waves of praise flowing continuously.

These are continuous waves of light, interconnected, so there are no pauses between them, because each one draws in the next [2], as if the apostle was expressing it while being filled with a wealth of emotions erupting from his heart with gratitude, blessings, and praise. He cannot stop this engulfing torrent that pours from his heart. This prayer could be considered a live example and model of the prayers of the early Church, especially the blessing prayers,[3] which were recited in the ritual of breaking bread, an early prototype of Mass.

The opening of this message: "Blessed be the God and Father of our Lord Jesus Christ," is repeated in more than one letter:

"Blessed be the God and Father of our Lord Jesus Christ, the Father of mercies and God of all comfort..." (2 Corinthians 1:3).

"Blessed be the God and Father of our Lord Jesus Christ, who according to His abundant mercy has begotten us again to a living hope through the resurrection of Jesus Christ from the dead..." (1 Peter 1:3).

---

[2] Notice the frequent occurrence of the relative pronoun "who" or "which", as it is repeated 11 times in these few lines.

[3] It is well known that the blessing is one of the four basic Eucharistic actions: taking, blessing, breaking, and giving. The Holy Mass still begins in this order. After the priest takes the offerings during the presentation of the lamb, he pronounces a blessing over them: "Blessed be God the Father, the ruler of all, Amen. Blessed be His only Son, our Lord Jesus Christ, Amen. Blessed be the Holy Spirit, the Comforter, Amen.

The Opening Anthem

These openings give us an idea about the prayers of the Apostles in the early Church and how they always began with blessing God, who is the Father of our Lord Jesus Christ.

The element of blessing and praise is a fundamental thing in the Christian life. The early Christians were always praising: "And they were continually in the temple, praising and blessing God"[4] . Their lives were an ongoing celebration filled with joy and exultation: "Rejoice in the Lord always. Again, I will say, rejoice!"[5] . But what were they rejoicing about? They rejoiced in the immense blessings and great favours they found themselves immersed in.

In Ephesians 1, starting from verse 3 to verse 14, it is like a spiritual melody, a symphony praising God's favours upon us. And like any symphony, it has a recurring theme. This recurring theme is: "for the praise of his glory," where this phrase is repeated three times in this passage:

In verse 6, it says: "to the praise of the glory of His grace, by which He made us accepted in the Beloved,"[6]

Then in verse 12: "that we who first trusted in Christ should be to the praise of His glory",[7]

And in verse 14: "(The Holy Spirit) who is the guarantee of our inheritance until the redemption of the purchased possession, to the praise of His glory."[8]

Therefore, the whole passage is set for the praise of God's glory. This is the end of all things, to which everything aspires, and what we will reach in the blissful eternity. But it is an extended end, open without limit, as we will continue eternally growing endlessly in praising and glorifying the divine glory. This praise is the ultimate goal of all the spiritual blessings given to us in Christ. Blessings before time, in the core of time, and at

---

4 Luke 24:53
5 Philippians 4:4
6 Ephesians 1:6
7 Ephesians 1:12
8 Ephesians 1:14

the end of times. It is noticeable that these blessings that St. Paul enumerates from verse 3 to verse 14, begin before the foundation of the world. While Christ was born in 4 BC, the blessings given to us in Christ precede that by a lot, not only before we existed or were created, but even before God created anything. The Word was in the Father's bosom, and the Word's incarnation was known in the Father's heart, so the Father saw in His intended incarnate Son the perfect human image. So, humanity was loved by the Father in the person of Christ, known to be incarnate since eternity. This is what Apostle Peter points out: "He indeed was foreordained before the foundation of the world, but was manifest in these last times for you"[9].

The first blessing in the series of blessings given to us in Christ is the choice: "just as He chose us in Him before the foundation of the world, that we should be holy and without blame before Him in love" (Ephesians 1:4).

The second blessing is predestination to adoption, meaning that adoption was prepared for us before we existed and even from eternity: "having predestined us to adoption as sons by Jesus Christ to Himself, according to the good pleasure of His will"[10].

These two blessings precede time, given to us in Christ before the creation began, in eternity.

There are blessings that came at the core of time, like redemption, when sin entered the world, as he says: "In him we have redemption through his blood"[11], and like the portion we obtained in Christ: "In him we have also obtained an inheritance"[12], and another similar word to it is inheritance: "(The Holy Spirit) who is the guarantee of our inheritance"[13].

The greatest blessing we have received in Christ is the Holy Spirit: "In Him you also trusted, after you heard the word

9 1 Peter 1:20
10 Ephesians 1:5
11 Ephesians 1:7
12 Ephesians 1:11
13 Ephesians 1:14

The Opening Anthem

of truth, the gospel of your salvation; in whom also, having believed, you were sealed with the Holy Spirit of promise" [14].

There are also eschatological blessings that come when times of relief arrive, times of the restoration of all things (Acts 3:19, 21), which he here calls the "plan for the fullness of time" and is the unifying of all things under one head in Christ (Ephesians 1:10). This is the final blessing, which he elaborates on in another letter saying that everything in the end will be subject to Christ, and Christ himself will subject everything to God the Father, "that God may be all in all" [15].

All of these are the spiritual blessings we have received in Christ, which the apostle delights in, one after the other, throughout these twelve verses, with feelings of praise and glorification that well up in his heart, demonstrating that all of them aspire and end in praising God's glory. This is the refrain that recurrently returns in this spiritual hymn.

"IN CHRIST" THE KEY PHRASE IN THE LETTER TO THE EPHESIANS

The magic word that introduced the Apostle into these sublime spiritual atmospheres, and that allows us to participate with him in feelings of praise, and without which we could not understand anything from the Letter to the Ephesians, is the phrase "In Christ." It is repeated, along with its synonyms like "in Him," "in the Beloved," "in that one," 11 times in this paragraph alone. In the first two chapters, it is repeated 22 times.

This repetition and this focus on the phrase reveal to us that the fundamental truth that filled the mind of Apostle Paul as he recited this spiritual hymn is that we are now immersed in a completely new environment unlike the one we used to live in.

---

14 Ephesians 1:13
15 1 Corinthians 15:28

We used to live in the world [16], but now we have become a new creation, we are "In Christ." This is a new mode of existence: "Therefore, if anyone is in Christ, he is a new creation; old things have passed away; behold, all things have become new."[17] The new creation's concise definition is: our existence in Christ. Christ is the new divine environment that now contains and engulfs us, and in which we now live. If we do not perceive this truth with our spirits, and not our minds, we will not be able to understand anything from the Letter to the Ephesians, and the divine blessings that are spoken about will remain mere words without a sense of their true spiritual magnitude. The choice, adoption, redemption, and complete unification will remain theoretical concepts that we cannot spiritually comprehend or understand because all of them happened and were given to us "In Christ."

Here are some key verses that include the phrase "In Christ" and its synonyms in the Letter to the Ephesians:

"Paul, an apostle of Jesus Christ by the will of God, To the saints who are in Ephesus, and faithful in Christ Jesus" [18]. Looking at the original Greek, we find that the word "faithful" here is not a participle but a noun[19]. So, it doesn't mean "those who believe in Christ," but "the believers who are in Christ Jesus." The focus is not on their faith in Christ, but on them being "in Christ Jesus." The intended meaning is that these believers are completely immersed in Christ, not just that Christ is the subject of their faith.

"Who has blessed us with every spiritual blessing in the heavenly places in Christ"[20]. Every "spiritual blessing" is given to us "in Christ." This verse seems to be a summary and index of all the following blessings given to us "in Christ."

---

16 Colossians 2:20 reads: "Therefore, if you died with Christ from the basic principles of the world..."
17 2 Corinthians 5:17
18 Ephesians 1:1
19 "It did not come to those who believe, but it came to the faithful."
20 Ephesians 1:3

The Opening Anthem

"Just as He chose us in Him before the foundation of the world..."[21]. He saw us in Him before time, loved our image in Christ, and chose to create us to be members in the body of His intended Son.

"Which He made us accepted in the Beloved."[22] Notice the big difference between saying "He lavished on us by the Beloved" or "through the Beloved," and "in the Beloved." This grace that was given to us was not just obtained through Jesus Christ, the beloved Son; it was in the beloved Jesus Christ. The Father saw us in His beloved Son Jesus, loved us as we exist in His Son, as if we were intertwined in Him or about to become members in Him, and He loved us.

"In Him we have redemption through His blood"[23]. Redemption is not only obtained by Him but in Him. Christ didn't give us redemption as a gift separate from Himself, but He gave us Himself, so we obtained redemption in Him. When we were baptised, joined His body, and became members of Him, immersed in His divine blood, we obtained redemption in Him, not just through Him. Christ is not just the means of redemption, and redemption is not just one of His gifts, but redemption is reserved for us in Him. We obtain it when we enter Him and become immersed in His divine blood.

"Having made known to us the mystery of His will, according to His good pleasure which He purposed in Himself"[24]. In the common translation, it says "which He purposed in Himself," but in the old manuscripts, it comes as "which He purposed in Him," meaning that the Father purposed that in His Son. This old reading agrees more with the context of the speech. In the previous verses, He said that the Father blessed us in Christ, chose us in Him, and in Him gave us redemption; and now, He says that the Father intended this good intention for us in His

---

21 Ephesians 1:4
22 Ephesians 1:6
23 Ephesians 1:7
24 Ephesians 1:9

IN HIM

Son. When He foresaw us in His Son, He was pleased with us, so He purposed all these good intentions for us in His Son.

"That in the dispensation of the fullness of the times He might gather together in one all things in Christ, both which are in heaven and which are on earth—in Him."[25] Everything in heaven and on earth will be brought together under one head "in Christ."

"In Him also we have obtained an inheritance, being predestined according to the purpose of Him who works all things according to the counsel of His will, that we who first trusted in Christ should be to the praise of His glory. In Him you also trusted, after you heard the word of truth, the gospel of your salvation; in whom also, having believed, you were sealed with the Holy Spirit of promise." [26]

Note that to hear and benefit from the gospel, we must be "in Christ." The gospel, like all blessings, is given to us "in Christ," and we must read it in Christ, with the mind of Christ: "But we have the mind of Christ" [27]. This verse can also mean, "Now you are in Him when you heard the word of truth, the gospel of your salvation," meaning that hearing the gospel is what places us in Christ and Christ in us: "If anyone loves Me, he will keep My word; and My Father will love him, and We will come to him and make Our home with him."[28]

We are sealed by the Holy Spirit "in Christ"[29] . We receive the Holy Spirit in Christ as members of His body. His name is Christ because He is anointed with the Holy Spirit on behalf of all humanity. Now humanity is anointed with the Holy Spirit in

---

25 Ephesians 1:10
26 Ephesians 1: 11-13
27 1 Corinthians 2:16
28 John 14:23
29 Saint Athanasius says: "When the Lord accepted the Holy Spirit, it was us who accepted Him through Him... And when it was said that He was anointed in His human nature, it is us who in Him received the anointing" (Against the Arians 1: 47 and 48).

Christ, as we receive from His anointing: "And of His fullness we have all received, and grace for grace."[30]

Up to now, we have encountered the phrase "in Christ" and its synonyms 12 times, and by the end of the second chapter, this number reaches 22 times. With this insistence and repetition, the apostle Paul wants to assure us that all blessings have been given to us because of our existence in Christ, whether our current actual existence or our predestined existence in Him since eternity. This is the main thread of all of Paul's teachings, not only in this letter but throughout his other letters.

Interestingly, this spiritual theological principle is not only mentioned by the Apostle Paul when he speaks in theology or theoretical teaching or contemplation[31] ; but also in practical ethical teaching, that is, in moral commandments for men, women, children, slaves, and masters, basing his guidance each time on the fact that they are "in Christ."

THE PHRASE "IN CHRIST" IN ETHICAL GUIDELINES

Generally, Apostle Paul builds his moral commandments on the fundamental fact that we have come to live "in the Lord": "This I say, therefore, and testify in the Lord, that you should no longer walk as the rest of the Gentiles walk..."[32] . What does "I testify in the Lord" mean? It means "I testify to that as being in the Lord, and you are also in the Lord." Therefore, you should live just as you are in Jesus, as befits those who are

---

30 John 1:16
31 Paul's epistles usually begin with a theological or theoretical section, followed by practical commandments, and then he concludes his letter with blessings of peace and spiritual greetings. We will see that the phrase "in Christ" fills the pages of his letters, not only in the contemplative theoretical part as we have seen so far, but also in the moral commandments, and even in the greetings and salutations, where he often uses the phrase "in Christ," and "in the Lord."
32 Ephesians 4:17

"in Jesus". "For you were once darkness, but now you are light in the Lord. Walk as children of light"[33].

On this basis, when addressing children, he says: "Children, obey your parents in the Lord, for this is right"[34] Here, obedience is "in the Lord," not merely for the Lord, or to please the Lord or out of fear of the Lord. So, what does it mean for children to obey their parents "in the Lord"? It means they obey them as they and their parents are members of the one body of the Lord. Just as the body's parts are submissive to each other in perfect harmony for the good of the whole body, so children should be submissive to their parents for the good of the body of Christ and love for the body's owner.

He applies this meaning in his letter to the Colossians to the relationship of the wife with her husband: "Wives, submit to your own husbands, as is fitting in the Lord."[35] , and there are many other examples in all the letters.

In fact, we say that even when he does not mention the phrase "in the Lord", all his moral teaching is based on the fact that Christ is the new medium in which we live. So, when he deals with a specific kind of sin, such as bodily sins, he speaks on the basis of this fact: "Do you not know that your bodies are members of Christ? Shall I then take the members of Christ and make them members of a harlot? Certainly not!"[36] Similarly, when addressing the problem of division and partisanship that plagued the Corinthian church, he reminds them that they are the body of Christ and asks them in astonishment: "Is Christ divided?"[37] That is, can Christ have two bodies so that you create two factions? Paul was horrified by the spirit of partisanship that had entered their midst, because it was a sin that struck at the core of the body of the Lord.

---

33 Ephesians 5:8
34 Ephesians 6:1
35 Colossians 3:18
36 1 Corinthians 6:15
37 1 Corinthians 1:13

The Opening Anthem
THE PHRASE "IN THE LORD" IN THE SIMPLEST MATTERS

What's interesting is that we see the phrase "in the Lord" used in the simplest of speech, indicating that Apostle Paul considered our daily life, with all its matters, to be conducted "in the Lord". For example, when the Apostle sends his greetings and salutations to a group of believers, it is "in the Lord!" Chapter 16 of the Letter to the Romans gives us a realistic spiritual image of the life of the first Christian community, men and women, and when we read this chapter, we feel as if we are living amongst them. The phrase "in Christ" or "in the Lord" appears 10 times in this chapter:

"I commend to you Phoebe our sister, who is a servant of the church in Cenchrea, that you may receive her in the Lord in a manner worthy of the saints, and assist her in whatever business she has need of you; for indeed she has been a helper of many and of myself also. Greet Priscilla and Aquila, my fellow workers in Christ Jesus, who risked their own necks for my life, to whom not only I give thanks, but also all the churches of the Gentiles. Likewise greet the church that is in their house. Greet my beloved Epaenetus, who is the first fruits of Achaia to Christ. Greet Mary, who laboured much for us. Greet Andronicus and Junia, my countrymen and my fellow prisoners, who are of note among the apostles, who also were in Christ before me. Greet Amplias, my beloved in the Lord. Greet Urbanus, our fellow worker in Christ, and Stachys, my beloved. Greet Apelles, approved in Christ. Greet those who are of the household of Aristobulus. Greet Herodion, my countryman. Greet those who are of the household of Narcissus who are in the Lord. Greet Tryphena and Tryphosa, who have laboured in the Lord. Greet the beloved Persis, who laboured much in the Lord. Greet Rufus, chosen in the Lord, and his mother and mine."[38]

---

38 Romans 16:2-13

Where did Saint Paul get this concept from? Where did the Apostle get this concept about our existence in Christ? And if he received it from the Lord, when and how did he receive it?

The truth is, this concept is intrinsic to the "mystery of Christ" that was "revealed by the Spirit"[39] and Paul advanced in its declaration until he reached a very high level of familiarity with it, as he himself says: "By revelation He made known to me the mystery (as I have briefly written already, by which, when you read, you may understand my knowledge in the mystery of Christ)". [40]

This revelation began powerfully since his first spiritual experience on the road to Damascus, which was the first and foundational experience in his life. He did not stop afterward from delving into its meaning and revealing its content, and it was the beginning of the inspiration that he received from the Lord about our new entity and existence in Christ, and about the Church which is His body.

The intensity of his impact from this incident is shown by the fact that he repeats it on every occasion. The story, in all its details, is repeated three times in the Acts of the Apostles: in Acts 9, Acts 22, and Acts 26.

"I persecuted this Way to the death, binding and delivering into prisons both men and women, as also the high priest bears me witness, and all the council of the elders, from whom I also received letters to the brethren, and went to Damascus to bring in chains even those who were there to Jerusalem to be punished. "Now it happened, as I journeyed and came near Damascus at about noon, suddenly a great light from heaven shone around me. And I fell to the ground and heard a voice saying to me, 'Saul, Saul, why are you persecuting Me?' So I answered, 'Who are You, Lord?' And He said to me, 'I am Jesus of Nazareth, whom you are persecuting.' "And those who were with me indeed saw the light and were afraid, but they

---

39 Ephesians 3:5
40 Ephesians 3:3-4

did not hear the voice of Him who spoke to me. So I said, 'What shall I do, Lord?' And the Lord said to me, 'Arise and go into Damascus, and there you will be told all things which are appointed for you to do.'" [41]

One of the most important details of this story is the phrase "shone around me", which is repeated in the three locations where this story is mentioned. An analysis of the word in Greek highlights the strength of this word more clearly[42] . The light that shone around him made the Apostle immersed within it. It was not merely a light he saw in front of him; it was a new luminary environment surrounding him. From the centre of this luminous environment, a voice came to him, saying: "Saul, Saul, why are you persecuting me?"[43] What is more surprising is that the Apostle realised that the Lord was the one speaking to him: "Who are you, Lord?" And He said to me, "I am Jesus, whom you are persecuting."[44] Paul was persecuting men and women and dragging them into prison. So how can the Lord say that Paul was persecuting Him? Is there such a close, existential relationship between the Lord and these men and women whom he was persecuting? Are they one entity with Jesus, who is speaking to him, the centre of this light?

This was the beginning of his realisation of the mystery of Christ. When he later learned that the Lord feeds these people with his body and blood, he understood. He understood why these people are one entity with the Lord: The Lord gave them His body to eat, so these men and women have the Lord's body in them. Therefore, whoever persecutes them is in fact persecuting the Lord personally, because he is persecuting His body. Thus, he began to realise the mystery of the divine body, in which is the unsearchable riches of Christ, the mystery of the

---

41 Acts 22:4-10
42 In Acts 9:3, περιήστραψεν is derived from περι- = around, and ἀστραπή = lightning In Acts 26:13, περιλάμψαν is derived from περι- = around, and λάμπω = to shine In Acts 22:6, which is the strongest of them, περι- is repeated twice: περιαστράψαι...περὶ ἐμέ
43 Acts 22:7
44 Acts 22:8

IN HIM

Church, which is His body, the fullness of Him who fills all in all. This is the revelation that the Lord unveiled to him: "how that by revelation He made known to me the mystery"[45]. "For I neither received it from man, nor was I taught it, but it came through the revelation of Jesus Christ."[46] From that moment, Paul began to grasp the truth of Christ and the reality of our existence in Him, and the Spirit increased his understanding, revelation, and knowledge of this mystery until this mystery possessed his entire being, filled his mind and heart, and dominated all his writings throughout all his epistles.

If we realised this mystery, if we truly lived it, if it ruled over our hearts as it ruled over the heart of Apostle Paul, then we would feel as if we were not living on earth. Yes, our existence here may be real on the visible level, but on the level of profound truth: we exist in Christ, we are immersed within the divine body, in the Church, which is His body, the fullness of Him who fills all in all. If we really feel this, then our hearts will be filled with joy and continuous praise, day and night.

This feeling is what our early ascetic fathers meant by the concept of "estrangement". Estrangement, like virginity, should not be understood in the negative sense but in the positive one. Virginity is a marital connection with Christ, and estrangement is belonging to the true homeland, heavenly Jerusalem, "the Church, which is His body, the fullness of Him who fills all in all."[47]

---

45 Ephesians 3:3
46 Galatians 1:12
47 Ephesians 1:23

CHAPTER

3

Blessed be the God and Father of our Lord Jesus Christ

The optimal way to meditate[1] is to take it word by word, repeating it in our mouths, understanding it with our hearts, and absorbing the spiritual value in it until we are fully satisfied, then we move to the next word, repeating it over and over, and then we take the two words together, and so on until the meanings of the words "piercing even to the division of soul and spirit, and of joints and marrow"[2].

"Blessed..."-

In Greek, it's eulogētós Εὐλογητός. It consists of two parts: eu-, which means good or beneficial or nice. And logētós derived from logos meaning: word or saying. So, the meaning would be: "deserving every good word, every praise, and every glorification."

"Blessed," this word can be considered the title of the entire letter. The whole letter to the Ephesians is written to praise the glory of God. The phrase "to the praise of his glory" is considered the refrain of this spiritual hymn and it is repeated 3 times. This letter is written to commend God's bounties and

---

[1] Tape number 40 dated November 16, 1989
[2] Hebrews 4:12

his overwhelming love with which he enveloped us. Indeed, Christianity is essentially a religion of praise. The early Church did not cease to praise. Saint Luke ends his Gospel with this verse: "And they were continually in the temple, praising and blessing God"[3] . The feeling of the early Christians that Christ loved us so much that he died for us, made us kings and priests with him to God his Father, elevated us, gave us a heavenly call, and made us partners in his glory with the Father. This overwhelming feeling made them unceasingly praising, day and night.

In fact, praising can be considered a sign of spiritual health; just as we say that a thermometer can measure physical health. The opposite of praising is grumbling. Grumbling is a sign of spiritual sickness. A person who constantly finds faults in circumstances and others, is spiritually sick. But a person who never stops praising, lives a life of gratitude, their eyes open to the immense glory given to us in Christ in heaven, this person is spiritually healthy. Praising is a sign that a person is not confined to himself. The prayer of request can be for personal benefit or for the success of what we do so that we can gain fame, and even the prayer of repentance and regret can be centred on the self, how did I commit such a sin? I repent not because I saddened God; but because my spiritual status has been demeaned by this mistake. But the prayer of praise is a sign that a person has freed himself from himself and has become only concerned with pleasing his beloved God, praising his God because He is good, kind, generous, holy, and glorious. This person's focus is God, His righteousness, His goodness, and he does not care about himself in anything.

"Blessed be God..." But who is God? God is the infinite spirit that fills the heavens and the earth, that permeates all existence, that spans time since before eternity, before angels existed, before God created anything, before He commanded "Let there be light", for an infinite time.

---

[3] Luke 24:53

Blessed be the God and Father of our Lord Jesus Christ

The simplest and most basic definition of God is the very simple verse: "God is love"[4]. God is an eternal love energy that existed before all ages, before the creation of the world in an infinite time, an infinite love energy poured from the Father into His beloved Son, and reciprocated from the beloved Son to the Father in the fellowship of the Holy Spirit. This is the simplest definition of God in His essence, regardless of His works in creation and all His benevolence towards it. As a result of the supreme eternal love energy between the Father and the Son, the heavens, the earth, and everything in them were created.

"THE FATHER OF OUR LORD JESUS CHRIST"

God is the absolute fatherhood, in Him is the original fatherhood. St. Paul says in the same letter: "I bow my knees to the Father of our Lord Jesus Christ, from whom the whole family in heaven and earth is named."[5] The word "fatherhood" in common translation came as "clan", which is originally πατριά from πατήρ = father, so it originally means "fatherhood" as it can also mean clan, on the basis that the clan belongs to one father, but from the context of the speech here it means "fatherhood".

The Heavenly Father is the absolute fatherhood, He is the Father, and every other fatherhood, whether it be physical earthly (like the fatherhood of the physical father) or spiritual on earth (like the fatherhood of the spiritual father) is derived from the original fatherhood, from the fatherhood of the Heavenly Father. He says: "from whom every family in heaven and on earth is named" because there are also heavenly families and all of them are also derived from the fatherhood of the Heavenly Father, who is the origin of all fatherhood, like the fatherhood of St. Macarius or the fatherhood of St. Anthony to all the monks of the world, or the fatherhood of St. Mark to the Egyptian Church, he is

---
4 1 John 4:16
5 Ephesians 3:14-15

the one who introduced us, Egyptians, to Christ, and like the fatherhood of Abraham "who is the father of us all" [6] because he is the father of faith.

All these fatherhoods, whether earthly or heavenly, their origin and source is God the Father, the owner of complete and absolute fatherhood, and the source of all true fatherhood in heaven and on earth. Therefore, blessed be God the Father, the Father in whom is the infinite paternal love, who gives each father a reflection and a spark of His fatherhood.

This phrase clarifies the meaning of God the Father's parenthood, significantly broadening the concept. The truth is, none of us truly knows the Father as He really is, and no one can know Him unless "the Son wills to reveal him"[7] . "No one has seen God at any time. The only begotten Son, who is in the bosom of the Father, He has declared Him."[8] He is the only one who can inform us about the Father and truly speak of Him.

Jesus, the only Son of God, has revealed the Father to us. He has unveiled His depths and shown them to mankind. But what is the message He gave us about the Father? "This is the message which we have heard from Him and declare to you, that God is light and in Him is no darkness at all."[9] . The Father is infinite light, absolute positivity, supreme love. He does not know how to hate or hold grudges, and there is no darkness in Him. The central message of Christ is to inform us about who the Father is[10]. At the core of His being, Christ is the revelation of the Father, the visible proclamation of the unseen Father[11]. Christ

---

6 Romans 4:16
7 Luke 10: 22
8 John 1:18
9 1 John 1:5
10 In fact, this includes all other aspects of the message of Christ: it includes reconciliation with the Father, and it includes liberation from sin: "And you shall know the truth (i.e., the truth of the Father), and the truth shall make you free" (John 8:32), and it includes the gift of eternal life: "And this is eternal life, that they may know You, the only true God..." (John 17:3).
11 This is what St. Irenaeus says: "The Father is the unseen truth of the Son, and the Son is the visible truth of the Father" (Against Heresies 4:6:6).

Blessed be the God and Father of our Lord Jesus Christ

Himself said, "The time is coming when I will no longer speak to you in figurative language, but I will tell you plainly about the Father."[12] . Note that Christ said this towards the end of His farewell discourse in John 16, then soon afterwards revealed what this "time" is, saying to the Father, "Father, the hour has come. Glorify Your Son, that Your Son also may glorify You"[13] . What is this "time" that He is speaking about in both verses? It is the hour of the cross. On the cross, Christ openly informed us about the Father's love for the world and that "God so loved the world that He gave His only Son..."[14].

So, when the apostle mentions Jesus Christ to define the nature of God the Father's parenthood he is reminding us of who this Father is. He is the Father "who did not spare his own Son, but delivered him up for us all"[15] . He is the Father who has shown us His depths through His sacrifice of His son Jesus, out of love for us.

On the other hand, mentioning the Father's parenthood towards Jesus Christ at the beginning of this hymn serves as a prelude to the main idea permeating the entire hymn, that the relationship between the Father and the Son is the source of all the blessings mentioned. All spiritual blessings are given to us by the Father through His beloved Son: the selection, the adoption, the redemption, the Gospel, the Holy Spirit. Christ is the medium through which all spiritual blessings from the Father has poured onto us. Therefore, it is very appropriate to praise God as the Father of our Lord Jesus Christ.

---

12 John 16:25
13 John 17:1
14 John 3:16
15 Romans 8:32

IN HIM
"...THE ONE WHO HAS BLESSED US WITH EVERY SPIRITUAL BLESSING..."

What is the concept of blessing? The term "blessing" has a concept in the Old Testament that is spread across all the books, but it mainly revolves around material abundance. So, when God blesses a person, it means that He greatly increases their earthly blessings. The first blessing said in the Old Testament was to Adam: "Then God blessed them, and God said to them, "Be fruitful and multiply; fill the earth""[16] . Then God blessed Noah after the flood: "So God blessed Noah and his sons, and said to them: "Be fruitful and multiply, and fill the earth.""[17] And He also blessed Abraham: "blessing I will bless you, and multiplying I will multiply your descendants as the stars of the heaven and as the sand which is on the seashore" [18]. Deuteronomy chapter 28 lists countless blessings that God gives to those who obey Him: " And all these blessings shall come upon you and overtake you, because you obey the voice of the Lord your God: "Blessed shall you be in the city, and blessed shall you be in the country. ""Blessed shall be the fruit of your body, the produce of your ground and the increase of your herds, the increase of your cattle and the offspring of your flocks. "Blessed shall be your basket and your kneading bowl.""[19]

All these blessings revolve around abundance and prosperity in everything. This is the primary concept of blessing in the Old Testament: richness and abundance in the earth's blessings due to God's favour of man; as if God was raising man while he was in spiritual infancy, in preparation for giving him spiritual blessings in the New Testament that are beyond measure.

The blessings of the New Testament, on the other hand, are more refined and elevated compared to those in the Old Testament. They are all spiritual, not material, and ultimately lead

---

16 Genesis 1:28
17 Genesis 9:1
18 Genesis 22:17
19 Deuteronomy 28: 2-5

Blessed be the God and Father of our Lord Jesus Christ

to spiritual fellowship with God. As our teacher Peter says, "His divine power has given to us all things that pertain to life and godliness, through the knowledge of Him who called us by glory and virtue, by which have been given to us exceedingly great and precious promises, that through these you may be partakers of the divine nature."[20] And as John the Apostle says, "Our fellowship is with the Father and with his Son, Jesus Christ."[21]. And as Paul the Apostle himself says, "God is faithful, by whom you were called into the fellowship of his Son, Jesus Christ our Lord."[22] This fellowship is not limited, but the growth in it is open to infinity, "with all the fullness of God."[23] Thus, man's highest calling and greatest blessing became "for the obtaining of the glory of our Lord Jesus Christ."[24] Notice that all these blessings entail entering into spiritual fellowship with God for eternal life.

St. John wrote his gospel under the urging of the elders of the Ephesian church, who were insistently asking when he came to reside with them: is what Paul taught us based on the sayings of the Lord? Or was Paul more bold than necessary? Are we really called to share in the glory of our Lord Jesus Christ? Can we truly be filled to all the fullness of God? Is this reasonable?

It's as if John replies to them, saying, 'Yes, I was sitting next to Him on the last night, and I heard Him praying to the Father, saying, "And the glory which You gave Me I have given them, that they may be one just as We are one"'[25] . Then I heard Him say to the Father, "that the love with which You loved Me may be in them, and I in them."[26] Christ Himself asked that the very same love with which the Father loved the Son be poured into our hearts. So, it's not an exaggeration or hyperbole when Paul

---

20 2 Peter 1:3-4
21 1 John 1:3
22 1 Corinthians 1:9
23 Ephesians 3:19
24 2 Thessalonians 2:14
25 John 17:22
26 John 17:26

says, "And to know the love of Christ, which passes knowledge, that you may be filled with all the fullness of God"[27], or when he says that "because the love of God has been poured out in our hearts by the Holy Spirit who was given to us." [28]

This is the level of blessing in the New Testament. To understand what he means here by saying "the one who has blessed us with every spiritual blessing,"[29] we must raise our minds above all that is on earth, and not let it be confined to the tangible blessings we have received.

Indeed, we should thank God for all the material blessings He has given us; we thank God for all His kindness. However, this is the most basic level, the level of the Old Covenant, which after fulfilling it, we must ascend to a much higher level, we must soar and ascend to the level of spiritual blessings in the heavenly realms. For He "raised us up together and made us sit together in the heavenly places in Christ Jesus" (Ephesians 2:6), so we could be "partakers in the heavenly calling"[30], because we are originally "called into fellowship of His Son, Jesus Christ"[31].

"WITH EVERY SPIRITUAL BLESSING"

The New Testament is filled with verses that describe God's gift to us as being complete, using the word "all":

"He who did not spare His own Son, but delivered Him up for us all, how shall He not with Him also freely give us all things?" (Romans 8:32).

"All things work together for good to those who love God" (Romans 8:28).

"He whoever overcomes will inherit all things" (Revelation 21:7)

---

27 Ephesians 3:19
28 Romans 5:5
29 Ephesians 1:3
30 Hebrews 3:1
31 1 Corinthians 1:9

Blessed be the God and Father of our Lord Jesus Christ

"Now to Him who is able to do exceedingly abundantly above all that we ask or think" (Ephesians 3:20), meaning no matter what spiritual blessings you ask for or imagine, God is capable of giving you even more than all your imaginings.

"That you may be filled with all the fullness of God" (Ephesians 3:19). Is there a greater totality than this?

"Very truly[32] I tell you, whatever you ask the Father in My name, He will give you" (John 16:23).

Ask what you wish, and God is ready it to give you, why? Because He has already given you what is greater than everything. Is there anything more valuable than His Son? His Son, who is infinitely more valuable than everything in heaven and on earth. The entire creation is worth nothing in front of the only beloved Son. "He who did not spare[33] His own Son, but delivered Him up for us all, how shall He not with Him also freely give us all things?"

In reality, those whose eyes are open to the richness of the blessings God has given us and showered us with in the New Covenant will never cease thanking and praising God. Their soul becomes overflowing with gratitude and praise at all times, and they experience profound feelings of gratitude, like the saints who said: You did not leave me lacking in any of Your works of majesty (Gregorian Mass); "I am filled with comfort. I am exceedingly joyful"[34]; "For all things are for your sakes, that grace, having spread through the many, may cause thanksgiving to abound to the glory of God."[35] Notice in these two verses the repetition and synonymy of expressions of gratitude and great increase. The Apostle wants to draw our attention to the

---

32 When Christ says, "Truly, truly, I tell you..." we must consider that He Himself is "the Truth" in an absolute sense, as if He is swearing by Himself, just as God swore by Himself to Abraham: "By myself I have sworn, says the Lord..." (Titus 22:16). Therefore, when Christ says: "Truly, truly, I tell you", all we have to do is say: "Amen, Amen".
33 "Did not spare" in the original Greek means "did not withhold from us", "did not reserve for us", "did not skimp on us".
34 2 Corinthians 7:4
35 2 Corinthians 4:15

abundance of grace which requires abundant thanksgiving, so that in the end it results in the glory of God.

The blessings of the New Covenant are called "spiritual" for two reasons:

1- Because they are inherently spiritual and not material, unlike the blessings of the Old Covenant.

2- Because they are given to us through the Spirit; the Holy Spirit is the one who delivers them to us.

Indeed, the Holy Spirit is entrusted to convey to us the richness of Christ. The main role of the Holy Spirit concerning us can be summed up in this verse: "He will glorify Me, for He will take of what is Mine and declare it to you."[36] The primary role of the Son is to reveal the Father. And the primary role of the Holy Spirit is to take what belongs to the Son and deliver it to us. If the blessings of the New Covenant are all included in fellowship with the Son: "God is faithful, by whom you were called into the fellowship of His Son, Jesus Christ our Lord."[37] ; then the Holy Spirit is the one who realizes this fellowship, as it's fundamentally the spirit of fellowship.[38] He is the one who takes what belongs to Christ and gives it to us, according to the Lord's saying[39], and He takes not only from the Son but also from the Father and delivers it to us, so the Lord inferred: "All things that the Father has are Mine. Therefore I said that He will take of Mine and declare it to you."[40] It is understood from this that the Holy Spirit initially takes from the Father. Thus, it was said that "the love of God (i.e., the love of the Father) has been poured out in our hearts by the Holy Spirit who was given to us."[41]

---

36 John 16:14
37 1 Corinthians 1:9
38 2 Corinthians 13:14
39 John 16:14
40 John 16:15
41 Romans 5:5

Blessed be the God and Father of our Lord Jesus Christ

Many Fathers believe that when Christ said: "that the love with which You loved Me may be in them, and I in them."[42] He was implicitly asking for the descent of the Holy Spirit upon us, as the Holy Spirit is the one who transfers the Father's love to us. And the Alexandrian Fathers generally consider in their explanation of the Lord's prayer in John 17 that it is a prayer for the descent of the Holy Spirit upon us. [43]

The Spirit is the one who reveals the truth of God to us: "For the Spirit searches all things, yes, the deep things of God."[44] That is, the depths of the relationship between the Father and the Son. And St. Paul follows up by saying, "Now we have received, not the spirit of the world, but the Spirit who is from God, that we might know the things that have been freely given to us by God."[45] What are the things freely given to us by God? They are that we have fellowship with God. That we partake in the prayer of love that the Son raises towards the Father: "And because you are sons, God has sent forth the Spirit of His Son into your hearts, crying out, 'Abba, Father!'"[46]

In short, the Holy Spirit is the one who gives us our heavenly inheritance; St. Paul is correct in describing the blessings of the New Covenant as "spiritual" blessings, meaning they are given to us by the Holy Spirit.

Finally, we notice in this verse that begins the message with a blessing from God that St. Paul implicitly mentions the Father, Son, and Holy Spirit. This matter is common in his style, as he often mentions the three persons of the Trinity, even in the context of speech, without detailing them. The ritual blessing followed to this day in all traditional churches is always with the

---

42 John 17:26
43 Saint Athanasius, in his explanation of this prayer, puts the following words in the mouth of the Lord: Work in them, O Father, and as you gave me to wear this body, bless them with your Spirit, so that they too in this Spirit may become one and be fulfilled in me (Against the Arians 3: 23).
44 1 Corinthians 2:10
45 1 Corinthians 2:12
46 Galatians 4:6

mention of the Trinity. It is in our Coptic Church: Blessed is God the Father, the pantocrator. Amen. Blessed is His only Son, our Lord Jesus Christ. Amen. Blessed is the Comforter, the Holy Spirit. Amen. This is the blessing that begins the prayers of the Mass and all the church sacraments.

"WITH ALL SPIRITUAL BLESSINGS IN THE HEAVENS"

Here's an emphasis on the difference between the blessings of the Old Covenant and those of the New Covenant: the former were material and on earth, while the latter are entirely spiritual in the heavens.

Indeed, the calling of a Christian, or humanity in general, is heavenly. God didn't create humans merely to live on earth, but to have an infinite heavenly inheritance. Our entire lives on earth are considered mere moments when compared to the eternal life we're invited to. Hence, we are "partakers of the heavenly calling." [47]

In the letter to Philippi, the author speaks about those who have deviated from the heavenly calling: "For many walk, of whom I have told you often, and now tell you even weeping, that they are the enemies of the cross of Christ...who set their mind on earthly things. For our citizenship is in heaven." [48]

The question here is, why is focusing our thoughts only on earthly matters considered enmity to the cross of Christ? The cross is what elevates us, it draws us upward. As the Lord said, "And I, if I am lifted up from the earth, will draw all peoples to Myself."[49] Implying his elevation on the cross, through which he attracts everyone upwards. So, if we keep ourselves tied to the dust of the earth, focusing all our interests on earthly things,

---

47 Hebrews 3:1
48 Philippians 3:18-20
49 John 12:32

we eat, sleep, and our lives hold no interest beyond the earthly, we thereby fail the purpose of the cross, and resist Christ's attraction which wants to draw us up. We become enemies of the cross of Christ. However, if we respond to this attraction and focus our interest on what is above, where Christ sits, we become collaborators with the cross of Christ and responsive to his upward pull.

In the same letter to Ephesus, it is stated that God "and raised us up together, and made us sit together in the heavenly places in Christ Jesus"[50]. Note that "raised us" is past tense, meaning it has already been achieved. Although its full realisation will be when we transition from this world, we are already, according to the logic of the spirit in the New Covenant, considered to be living in the heavens. Thus, matters of the afterlife are present in spirit from now on, as the Lord said, "The hour is coming..."[51].

"Seek those things which are above, where Christ is, sitting at the right hand of God. Set your mind on things above, not on things on the earth." (Col 3:1-2). What is 'above' where Christ sits at the right hand of God, that we should be concerned with it? In truth, the only thing 'above' is the supreme mutual love relationship between the Father and the only Son. This paternal and filial love is what fills the heavens, around which the praises of angels and saints revolve, and they also partake in it. This is the joy of heaven. This is what the Apostle strongly and repeatedly urges us to seek and care about. In fact, the Apostle Paul's appeal to be concerned with what is above where Christ sits at the right hand of the Father, is rooted in the urgency of the Lord himself, his heart's desire, his prayer for us, and his greatest joy:

"Father, I desire that they also whom You gave Me may be with Me where I am, that they may behold My glory which You have given Me; for You loved Me before the foundation of the world." [52]

---

50 Ephesians 2:6
51 John 5:25
52 John 17:24

Christ's greatest desire is for us to see His glory. And what is His glory? His glory is that He has been loved by the Father from eternity, His glory is the eternal love poured out from the Father onto the Son. Note that Christ said this prayer just before He went directly to the cross. It is well-known that the last words uttered by any martyr before his death are considered a summary of his spirituality and his purpose for martyrdom. So, in the utmost sense, these are the final words of the Lord Jesus, they crystallise for us His purpose for the cross.

This is exactly what the Apostle Paul urges us to care about, saying: " Seek those things which are above, where Christ is, sitting at the right hand of God."[53] What is the meaning of "at the right hand of God"? God does not have a physical right and left[54] because He fills all places and transcends time and space. But the content of this statement is spiritual. It means that Christ has regained – or in a new way due to the body he wore, and thus for our sake – he regained his status with the Father, his eternal glory, and the love that was his before the creation of the world in the bosom of the Father. It is this love that Paul the Apostle urges us to seek and care about, and it is what Christ prayed for us. He wants us to be with him where He is so that we may witness this love - or this glory - and share in it.

---

53 Colossians 3:1

54 When the Son sits at the right hand of the Father, He does not thereby place the Father on His left!... but when the Son sits on the right, He sees the Father also on His right, as He says: "I foresaw the Lord always before my face, for He is on my right hand, that I should not be moved." From this, it becomes clear that as the Son is in the Father, so also is the Father in the Son, for when the Father is on the right, the Son is also on the right, and when the Son sits on the right, the Father is in the Son! Saint Athanasius the Apostolic, Against the Arians 1: 61 PG 26, 140

Blessed be the God and Father of our Lord Jesus Christ
"WITH EVERY SPIRITUAL BLESSING IN THE HEAVENS IN CHRIST"

This verse, with which this hymn begins, and especially the phrase "in Christ", is considered an index or summary of all the blessings that will be enumerated in the following verses, all of which are given to us "in Christ", i.e., because of the Father's love for the Son, and hence His love for us through His love for the Son.

But one might ask, what do we have to do with the Father's love for the Son? And how do we become beloved to the Father because of His love for the Son?

To understand this, we must first understand the mystery of the Incarnation. In His incarnation, Christ acquired humanity, united with human nature, thus establishing a mystical relationship[55], due to His participation in our nature, with every individual of this nature. Christ then came to represent all humanity before the Father. Hence, due to the incarnation, the Father's love for the Son now includes all members of human nature that were honoured by the Son of God's incarnation in them. Indeed, the Incarnation had a retroactive effect in eternity, as it was known from eternity that Christ would incarnate (1 Peter 1:20, Acts 15:18). Therefore, the image of His humanity was beloved to the Father from eternity, and hence we were loved through it before we existed.[56]

We are not beloved to the Father except through His love for His only Son. Because the Father is the only Father of an only Son, and the Son is the only Son (monogenes) of a Father who

---
[55] Indeed, Saint Cyril the Great believes that we had a mysterious existence in Christ: "We were all in Him because He became human, so He accepted the Spirit on our behalf to sanctify all human nature" (Interpretation of John 1: 32 and 33). "We were all in Christ and the human personality, in its entirety, was formed in Him" (Interpretation of John 1: 14).
[56] Saint Athanasius comments on Ephesians 1:4, saying: "How did God choose us in Him (in Christ) before we came into existence, unless we were predestined in Him?" (Against the Arians 2:76).

has no other son, and He is His only beloved. There is nothing beloved to the Father outside His only Son. In the only Son, Christ, all the infinite love energies in the Father's heart are focused, poured into the only Son from eternity and before the foundation of the world.

So how can we say that "God so loved the world"[57], if He loves nothing but His only Son? The truth is that God created everything through His only Son: "all things were made through him"[58], meaning that everything was created through the Father's relationship with the Son, through the Father's love for the Son. Consequently, it is inevitable that all creation is beloved to the Father, because it was created through the Son. The Father looks at creation and sees in it the mould that He shaped through the Son, and His love for His Son is reflected on that creation.

A READING FROM THE BOOK "FAITH IN CHRIST" BY OUR SPIRITUAL FATHER (FATHER MATTHEW THE POOR)

"Without Jesus Christ and without his mediation, it would be impossible for human nature to approach God or for his mercy to be poured into it. In Christ Jesus, all the absolute love of God the Father, all his absolute mercy, and all his absolute fatherhood with its glory and honour, have been poured out. Therefore, without Christ and outside of him, God has no love or mercy or fatherhood for any human, and not even life."[59]

However, someone might interpret this to mean that only Christians are loved by God, and the rest of humanity is not shown mercy or love by God. Of course, this is not correct. What this means is that everyone is loved by God the Father because of his love for his only Son. All creation, not just humanity, is loved by God the Father because it was created through his beloved

---

57 John 3:16
58 John 1:3
59 Faith in Christ by Father Matthew the Poor, Page 6.

Blessed be the God and Father of our Lord Jesus Christ

Son. On a higher level: Humanity is loved not just because it was created through the only Son, but because of the incarnation of the only Son and his union with human nature. Therefore, the image of every human, regardless of whether they are a believer or non-believer, good or evil, is very much loved by the Father, because Jesus Christ assumed this image, because the Son united with this humanity, and this nature became more beloved to the Father than the nature of angels and all other heavenly or earthly natures. Why? Because the Father now looks at a human and sees the image of his Son, the incarnated Word.

In another place in the book "Faith in Christ", Fr Matthew talks about the characteristics of love in the Father, and the characteristic of obedience in the Son: "The attributes of love and obedience in the divine essence are not closed to themselves in the Father and the Son, but are overflowing with vast goodness onto creation, just like the other attributes of God!.. And so, the Father loved the world through his love for his Son." [60]

"The fatherly love in the essence of God overflows onto all creation! God is the father of all creation, he loves it with an active paternal love. That is because his inherent love for his son is unlimited and not confined, it encompasses all creation." [61]

The Father is the only father to the only Son, and all the love of the Father was poured into the only Son, and all creation became loved by the Father through his love for Jesus. We are only blessed, chosen, and loved since eternity in Christ, and this is much stronger and steadier than being loved for ourselves. We are loved as members of the body of Christ. The Father began to love us in Christ as he loves Christ: "And You have loved them as You have loved Me." [62]

---

60 Ibid, 61
61 Ibid, 8
62 John 17:23

IN HIM
QUOTE FROM SAINT ATHANASIUS

"The Father finds His delight in the Son (Matthew 3:17), and with the same joy, the Son delights in the Father, saying: 'I was daily His delight, rejoicing always before Him' (Proverbs 8:30). This also confirms that the Son is not alien to the Father's essence, but is of this very essence. For God does not need to manufacture an external reason to delight in. Rather, the words here point to something that is intrinsic to God and equivalent to Him. When was the Father ever without joy? And if He is eternally joyful, then the subject of His joy must also be eternal. With what does the Father delight, if not by seeing Himself in His unique image, which is the Word (Logos)? And if after completing the creation of the world, He also delights in human beings, as is also written in the Book of Proverbs[63] , this agrees with the meaning of the first verse (i.e., 'I was daily His delight'), as He rejoices in them not by introducing into Himself another joy (alien to the first joy), but by seeing in them the likeness that was formed according to His unique image (which is the Son). Hence, even this joy that God delights in from us is also because of His delight in His unique image (which is the only begotten Son who sees us through Him)." [64]

To understand this discourse, we need to know the background behind it. Saint Athanasius was addressing the Arians, whose approach was to highlight the shared attributes between us and Christ to deduce that as we are created, so is the Son.

They claimed that if the Father delights in the Son, and then also says, "My delight is with humankind," then we are faced with two possibilities: either we are eternal like the Son, or the Son is created like us. This was the Arian objection. But Saint Athanasius' response was exquisite. He says that all our privileges are given to us "in Christ", we are loved by the Father because of His love for Christ, and if He delights in us, this joy is also

---

63 The following verse directly refers to: "And I was with mankind" (Proverbs 8:31
64 Against Arianism 2:82.

Blessed be the God and Father of our Lord Jesus Christ

because of His delight in His unique image (which is Christ) that He sees in us. This aligns with what we read in the book "Faith in Christ": "All the Father's love is poured into the only begotten Son, but the attributes of love and obedience within the divine essence are not confined to the Father and the Son, they overflow with profound goodness onto all creation, like the rest of God's attributes!.. and so the Father loved the world through His love for His Son."

THE FOURTH CHAPTER [65]
"HE CHOSE US IN HIM BEFORE THE FOUNDATION OF THE WORLD..."

The Epistle to the Ephesians, in general, and especially the verse we are currently discussing, is considered one of the New Testament passages that gives us a clear vision of the purpose of our life and the goal for which God brought us from non-existence into existence. Why did God create us? Where do we come from, and where are we going? What is the origin of our existence and what is the goal to which this existence leads? Is human life merely about living today like yesterday, eating, drinking, and sleeping until we are cast into the grave and thus our life ends?

Knowing the purpose of our existence, where we come from, and where we are going, gives us spiritual strength and clarity in our objectives. If the vision becomes blurred and the goal fades, life becomes meaningless, tasteless, and one may feel that their life is worthless. One may even reach the point of ending their own life, as they find no meaning in it.

The Epistle to the Ephesians shows us the extent of the spiritual wealth to which we are called "in the heavenly places in Christ". It rescues us from the whirlpool of earthly concerns that take up a large part of our time and interest, to reveal to us the wealth of

---
[65] Tape number 41 dated November 23, 1989

the heavens that are now offered to us and which we will enjoy for all eternity.

"Just as He chose us in Him before the foundation of the world, that we should be holy and without blame before Him in love."

[66]"Kathos..." connects the current discourse with the previous verse, making the meaning something like: "As an example of the spiritual blessings with which God has blessed us in Christ, we present the first of these blessings, which is: choice."

"He chose us in Him..." This choice pertains to all humanity and not one person over another. This means that God chose all humanity in Christ before the foundation of the world. He chose to create all humanity.

But what does it mean that this choice was made "in Him"?

When Christ incarnated, he acquired human nature in Himself, so the image of humanity became beloved to the Father because of His Son who took this image and wore it. Therefore, humanity became chosen in Christ due to Christ's incarnation.

True, Christ did not incarnate in the womb of the Virgin except "when the fullness of the time had come"[67] but it was known to the Father before the foundation of the world that the Son would become incarnate. The Apostle Peter says that we were bought "Knowing that you were not redeemed with corruptible things, like silver or gold, from your aimless conduct received by tradition from your fathers, but with the precious blood of Christ, as of a lamb without blemish and without spot. He indeed was foreordained before the foundation of the world, but was manifest in these last times for you."[68] Therefore, the image of His incarnation was known and beloved to the Father "before the foundation of the world", and because of that, we were known, chosen, and beloved by the Father in this image before we existed.

66 Ephesians 1:4
67 Galatians 4:4
68 1 Peter 1:18-20

Blessed be the God and Father of our Lord Jesus Christ

Recall the words of St. Athanasius commenting on this verse "He chose us in Him": How did He choose us (God) in Him before we came into existence, unless we were previously outlined in Him προτετυπωμένοι ἐν αὐτῷ. [69]

If we removed the word 'in Him' from the verse, the whole verse would fall apart, meaning we ourselves were not known, not chosen, not beloved, and we had no existence or mention before we were created, and indeed before the world was established. We were not supposed to be created in the first place. But all these blessings and gifts were given to us because of the Father's love for the Son before the establishment of the world, and his foreknowledge of incarnation.

'Chosen us in Him before the foundation of the world' implies that the choice applies to all humanity, not to one individual over another, because everyone is chosen 'in Christ' not in himself.

Christ is the 'Chosen One' in an absolute sense. In the Gospel of Matthew, the Father says about Him: "Behold! My Servant whom I have chosen"[70]. Moreover, during the Transfiguration, the verse (Luke 9:35) in the earliest manuscripts, as well as in the Bohairic and Sahidic Coptic translations, reads: 'This is my Chosen Son,' which is precisely equivalent to the common reading 'This is my beloved Son' found also in the Gospels of Matthew and Mark (Matthew 17:5; Mark 9:7). This is because the chosen one is the beloved; choice equates love, and my chosen Son is equivalent to my beloved Son. We were chosen in Him because He loved us in Him.

We are all chosen in Christ, but what distinguishes one from another is not the choice, but how much we strive to affirm this choice: "Therefore, brethren, be even more diligent to make your call and election sure, for if you do these things you will never stumble"[71]. A person being chosen doesn't mean that they have become holy and do not need to strive, of course, this is

---
69 Against Arianism 2:76
70 Matthew 12:18
71 2 Peter 1:10

an incorrect understanding. But if the chosen one doesn't strive, their choice is not stable, and they benefit nothing from their choice. But if they strive to affirm this choice, then they truly benefit from their choice.

CHAPTER

4

Just as He chose us in Him before the foundation of the world

There are several other verses in the New Testament that speak about what we received 'before the foundation of the world':

"In hope of eternal life which God, who cannot lie, promised before time began."[1] How did God promise before the ages began? To whom was this promise made? Did God make this promise to nothingness? To non-existence? Or who existed before the ages began to receive this promise? The only solution is that this promise came from the Father to the Son, because only the Father and the Son, in communion with the Holy Spirit, existed before the ages. Out of His infinite love for the Son and his foreknowledge of the incarnation, the Father promised the Son from the timeless ages that He would give us eternal life as an honour to His beloved Son. This fits perfectly with the verse: 'Just as He chose us in Him before the foundation of the world,' for when the Father saw us in Christ before the timeless ages, because of His foreknowledge of the incarnation, He chose us

---

1 Titus 1:2

in Christ, loved us in Him, and promised Christ that He would give us eternal life.

"Who has saved us and called us with a holy calling, not according to our works, but according to His own purpose and grace which was given to us in Christ Jesus before time began."[2] This means that this purpose and grace were given to us before we existed, and that was 'in Christ Jesus,' for He existed before the ages began to receive from the Father this purpose, this grace, and this promise of eternal life. And all this is because of the Father's love for His beloved Son before the creation of the world: "For You loved me before the foundation of the world."[3]

"Come, you blessed of My Father, inherit the kingdom prepared for you from the foundation of the world."[4] How could this kingdom have been prepared since the foundation of the world if not for the Father's love for the Son, who is the only truth that existed before the foundation of the world?

"HE CHOSE US IN HIM. TO BE HOLY AND BLAMELESS IN LOVE."[5]

We are chosen for holiness, to be holy. Every human being God created, He chose in Christ before the foundation of the world to be holy, and to live in perfect love, blameless before God. This is the selection of humanity, this is the original call of humanity, this is God's purpose in creating man.

From here we know where we came from and where we are going. We came from God's eternal purpose before the foundation of the world, we came from our existence in the heart of God prior to our actual existence in the world, and we are going to fulfill this calling and this choice in eternal life, to be holy and

---

2 2 Timothy 1:9
3 John 17:24
4 Matthew 25:34
5 Ephesians 1:4

Just as He chose us in Him before the foundation of the world blameless before God in love for eternity. God did not create us to live in dust for these limited years on earth.

God chose us and loved us in Christ before the foundation of the world, so He created us to be holy and perfect in the love of the Father, and to share in Christ's blameless position before God in love.

"He chose us in Him ... to be holy and without blame before Him in love."[6] Each of these phrases is linked to the phrase 'in Him' and can only be realised in Christ. Without Christ, we can't be holy and we can't be blameless or perfect, because man has a fallen nature, and perfection is foreign to his nature, so it is impossible to find a perfect human being on earth. Any person who seems to you to be holy and righteous, if you approach him a little, you will find that he is weak and has faults in himself. So, we are not holy but blameworthy in ourselves, and we have no right to show off before God, and we have no way to the love that is of God's nature; only 'in Him', in Christ, who alone is holy: "As He who called you is holy, you also be holy in all your conduct"[7]. Christ is "holy, harmless, undefiled, separate from sinners, and has become higher than the heavens"[8], and in Him alone we are sanctified because He "who became for us wisdom from God—and righteousness and sanctification and redemption"[9], and He said: "for their sakes I sanctify Myself, that they also may be sanctified by the truth."[10]

'And blameless...' ἀμώμους Christ alone is the one who is blameless: "as of a lamb without blemish and without spot"[11] (or blameless, ἀμώμου).

---

6 Ephesians 1:4
7 1 Peter 1:15
8 Hebrews 7:26
9 1 Corinthians 1:30
10 John 17:19
11 1 Peter 1:19

IN HIM
"BEFORE GOD"

This is Christ's eternal, existential position. Christ, in His essence, is before the Father and directed towards the Father. "In the beginning was the Word, and the Word was with God"[12], where 'with' in Greek is πρός, which means 'directed towards'. So, Christ in His eternal position as the Word, was continually directed towards the Father. The Father looks at Him and sees in Him, as in a mirror, a complete image of His paternal love, He sees in Him a filial love, an integrated image of His paternal love. "No one has seen God at any time. The only begotten Son, who is in the bosom of the Father, He has declared Him."[13] The phrase 'in the bosom of the Father' comes in Greek with the letter εἰς which means 'direction towards'. The Son in the bosom of the Father is not in a static (still) position; but in a dynamic position, continually directed towards and responding to the Father. This is Christ's eternal position towards the Father, and this is what we are called to 'in Christ': to dwell at every moment of our lives and in eternal bliss 'before God'. This constant existence in the presence of God is the fundamental human call for which God created him.

From the early times of the Old Testament, God called man to: "Walk before Me, and be blameless" (Genesis 17:1). And at the beginning of the New Testament, the Holy Spirit inspired Zechariah, father of John the Baptist, that the goal of the Messiah's message would be: "that we, Being delivered from the hand of our enemies, Might serve Him without fear, In holiness and righteousness before Him all the days of our life."[14] It's notable how similar this verse is to the one being explained. The Spirit who inspired Zechariah what the message of the Messiah would be, is the same one who announced to Apostle Paul what is the purpose of our calling in Christ. Indeed, it is the same one who announced to Saint John in the vision what our position

---
12 John 1:1
13 John 1:18
14 Luke 1:74-75

Just as He chose us in Him before the foundation of the world
would be in eternal happiness: "Therefore they are before the throne of God, and serve Him day and night"[15] . "They shall see His face, and His name shall be on their foreheads." [16]

So, we will dwell forever before the Father, participating in the filial love that Christ presents to His good Father from eternity to eternity.

"IN LOVE"

Christ in His eternal position is an infinite energy of filial love responding to the Father's love. And the highest calling of mankind is to participate with Christ in His response to the Father's love with filial feelings: "God is faithful, by whom you were called into the fellowship of His Son, Jesus Christ our Lord." [17]

"And because you are sons, God has sent forth the Spirit of His Son into your hearts, crying out, "Abba, Father!""[18]

This blameless filial love is what we are called to share with Christ, and it is the last thing Christ asked for us in His last prayer before He advanced to the cross: "that the love with which You loved Me may be in them, and I in them"[19], meaning that the eternal, infinite reciprocal love between the Father and the Son may be in us. This is the purpose for which human nature was created.

From the sayings of the Fathers about being in Christ before the foundation of the world:

By St. Athanasius the Apostolic[20]:

"Although the grace given to us by the Savior has 'now appeared,' as the apostle says (Titus 2:11), and came to us when the Savior

---

15 Revelation 7:15
16 Revelation 22:4
17 1 Corinthians 1:9
18 Galatians 4:6
19 John 17:26
20 Against the Arians 2:75-76 by St Athanasius

dwelt among us, this grace was prepared for us before we existed, and even before the foundation of the world!... And this is what the blessed apostle Paul teaches in his writings, saying: '...not because of our works but because of his own purpose and grace, which was given us in Christ Jesus before the ages began' (2 Timothy 1:9) And to the Ephesians: 'Blessed be the God and Father of our Lord Jesus Christ, who has blessed us in Christ with every spiritual blessing in the heavenly places, even as he chose us in him before the foundation of the world, that we should be holy and blameless before him in love' (Ephesians 1:4).

How then were we chosen before we came into existence unless we were – according to his saying – previously outlined in Him, 'predestined in him' before we existed!"

"And how did we receive grace 'before the eternal ages' when we did not exist, for we came into existence afterward in time, how did we receive that before the eternal ages unless the grace that was shown to us was stored up for us in Christ?"

"And so also on the day of judgment when everyone will receive according to his works he will say: 'Come, you who are blessed by my Father, inherit the kingdom prepared for you from the foundation of the world' (Matthew 25:34). How then was it prepared for us before we existed except in the Lord who was made for us before the ages a foundation, that we might be built upon him like well-fitted stones, and receive from him the life and grace that is in him!"

"In love he predestined us for adoption to himself as sons through Jesus Christ" (Ephesians 1:5)

"In love he predestined us..."- προορίσας ἡμᾶς

"In love": In Arabic, this phrase is used to establish the connection between the current sentence and the previous one. This connection in the original Greek is very close, as the current sentence comes with a subject referring back to the

Just as He chose us in Him before the foundation of the world
subject of the previous sentence. So, the literal translation would be "Having predestined us for adoption". Thus, the meaning of the two verses together would be: He chose us in him before the foundation of the world - how? - by predestining us for adoption. That is, adoption is the explanation and confirmation of our previous choice in Christ. It's not a new, independent meaning, but it clarifies the content of the choice in a clearer and more specific form.

"He predestined us for adoption..." What is meant by "adoption"?

Sonship in God is a hypostatic attribute of the Word of God, the Only Son. And adoption is to partake in His Sonship to the Father, because we are primarily called to fellowship with the Only Son, Jesus Christ: "God is faithful, by whom you were called into the fellowship of His Son, Jesus Christ our Lord."[21]

The essence of the Only Son's sonship is the filial love that He eternally offers to His Father: "But that the world may know that I love the Father"[22]. The essence of adoption is entering into the fellowship of this love. Saint John explains adoption and birth from God as entering into this love: "Everyone who loves is born of God and knows God"[23].

If you love, this is a sign that you have been born of God. You cannot love with a sincere, holy love without being born of God. If you do not love, this is a sign that your birth from God is not yet complete.

Love is God's nature. The simplest definition of God is "God is love"[24]. Therefore, God is the source of all genuine love. The beginning of the previous verse is: "Beloved, let us love one another, for love is of God; and everyone who loves is born of God and knows God."[25]

---

21 1 Corinthians 1:9
22 John 14:31
23 1 John 4:7
24 1 John 4:7,16
25 1 John 4:7

"Behold what manner of love the Father has bestowed on us, that we should be called children of God!"[26] That is, observe how the Father has poured love into us so that we might be called children of God. Here too, the love within us from God is evidence of being born of God.

"Therefore be imitators of God as dear children. And walk in love, as Christ also has loved us and given Himself for us, an offering and a sacrifice to God for a sweet-smelling aroma." [27]

What does this verse mean? The initial phrase "as dear children" suggests that the verse aims to explain the meaning of being adopted by God. The rest of the verse then shows that adoption fundamentally involves imitating Christ in offering himself to God out of love "an offering and a sacrifice to God for a sweet-smelling aroma." Therefore, adoption in its deepest sense is to participate with the Only Son in his complete love which he offers to the Father.

Does that mean we will be children of God just like Christ, the Only Son? And how then can he be the Only Son, the Monogenēs?

The truth is that Christ has two distinct titles which must be considered together: the title "Only Son" μονογενής as mentioned in John 1:18: "No one has seen God at any time. The only begotten Son, who is in the bosom of the Father, He has declared Him."[28], and the title "firstborn among many brethren" as mentioned in Romans 8:29: "For whom He foreknew, He also predestined to be conformed to the image of His Son, that He might be the firstborn among many brethren."[29] So, how can he have many siblings and still remain the Only Son? The truth is that when we become children of God, we are not additional sons alongside the Only Son, but rather we become sons from within the Only Son, in the Only Son. To the extent of our

---

26 1 John 3:1
27 Ephesians 5:1-2
28 John 1:18
29 Romans 8:29

Just as He chose us in Him before the foundation of the world

affiliation with the true, Only Son, Jesus Christ, we are only in Him sons of God. And to the extent of our involvement with Christ and our partnership with Him, only to that extent are we counted as children of God. We are not, of ourselves, children of God, because there is only one Son by nature, and we only participate in His unique Sonship to God from within Him.

"There's no such thing as adoption without the true Son who said, "No one knows the Father except the Son and those to whom the Son chooses to reveal him". All those called sons and gods (metaphorically) on Earth or in Heaven have attained sonship and divinity (relatively) through the Word. Everyone has obtained this through Him because He precedes everyone, and He is the only true Son, the only true God from the true God!"[30]

"ADOPTION THROUGH JESUS CHRIST HIMSELF"

All blessings are given to us in Christ and through Christ. But we notice here that mentioning Jesus Christ not only determines the way we obtain adoption (i.e., Christ is not just the one who gives us adoption), but it also largely determines the quality of this adoption. It's an adoption of a similar nature to Christ's unique sonship with God. It is "similar" not "equal" because Christ's sonship with God is unique and creation can't equate it, but it can resemble it: " For whom He foreknew, He also predestined to be conformed to the image of His Son, that He might be the firstborn among many brethren."[31]

So, the adoption "through Jesus Christ" is adoption of a particular nature, first by being a nature similar (but not equal) to Jesus Christ's unique sonship with God, and secondly, it comes only through our involvement with Jesus Christ, through sharing in Christ's filial feelings, through Christ's indwelling in us and the

---

30 St Athanasius the apostolic, against Arianism 1:39
31 Romans 8:29

pouring out of His filial love into our hearts: "The love of God has been poured out in our hearts by the Holy Spirit who was given to us."[32]

We ourselves can't love God with a filial love that befits God with our earthly hearts created from the dust. We might be able to love creation, creatures, and earthly things, but to love God with a love of His nature or befitting Him, this is not within the reach of our natural human capabilities: "Flesh and blood cannot inherit the kingdom of God"[33], where the essence of the kingdom of God is our entry into the realm of the divine love exchanged between the Father and the Son. It is impossible for flesh and blood, which are from the dust of the earth, to participate in the love between the Father and the Son. "Those who are in the flesh cannot please God"[34], but this is only given to us through Christ dwelling in us, and the Spirit of Christ dwelling in our hearts.

"And because you are sons, God has sent forth the Spirit of His Son into your hearts, crying out, "Abba, Father!""[35] This is one of the beautiful verses in which Apostle Paul mentions the Father, the Son, and the Holy Spirit implicitly within the context of the speech. And its meaning is that by the "Spirit of His Son" dwelling in us, we have entered into the heart of the relationship that binds the Father to the Son, so the love of the Son which He presents to the Father ascends from within our hearts with the Holy Spirit, who is the Spirit of the Son. And this is the deepest meaning of adoption through Jesus Christ.

Here are some quotes from the Church Fathers about adoption through Jesus Christ:

From Saint Athanasius the Apostolic: "We are not children of God by nature, but this is specific to the Son of God within us. Likewise, God the Father is not our father by nature, but He is

---

32 Romans 5:5
33 1 Corinthians 15:50
34 Romans 8:8
35 Galatians 4:6

Just as He chose us in Him before the foundation of the world the Father of the Word (Logos) within us, through whom we cry 'Abba, Father'. Thus, those whom the Father sees His own Son in, He also calls His children."[36]

From Saint Cyril the Great: "When the Father sees the features of His own Son, born of Him, clearly in us, He loves us also as His children, glorifies us, and shines on us with the honors surpassing this world."[37]

From Saint Athanasius the Apostolic: "Since the Word took our flesh and dwelt within us, therefore, because of the Word that is in us, God is called our Father."[38]

From Saint Cyril the Great: "Just as all fatherhood in heaven and on earth comes from the Father, for He alone is the Father in truth and absolutely (Ephesians 3:15), so too all sonship comes through the Son, for He alone is the Son in truth and absolutely."[39]

---

[36] Against Arianism 2:59, St Athanasius
[37] The Tenth Paschal Homily (from the year 422 AD) PG 77, 617-620, St Cyril the Great
[38] Defense of the Nicene Creed: 31, St Athanasius
[39] Commentary on the Gospel of John 1:34 PG 73, 213, St Cyril the Great

CHAPTER

5

To Unite all Things in Christ

THE FUNDAMENTAL VERSE IN SAINT IRENAEUS' THEOLOGY[1]

This verse was beloved by Saint Irenaeus to the extent that he made it the foundation of his theological teachings. The verse appears in the opening hymn of the Epistle to the Ephesians: "having made known to us the mystery of His will, according to His good pleasure which He purposed in Himself, that in the dispensation of the fullness of the times He might gather together in one all things in Christ, both which are in heaven and which are on earth—in Him."[2]

The crux of this verse is the phrase "gather together in one all things in Christ". The Greek word for "gather together" here, ἀνακεφαλαιώσασθαι, is a favourite term of Saint Irenaeus, and he used it more than 50 times in his writings[3] . Its overall meaning

---

1 A sermon dated November 26, 1987
2 Ephesians 1:9-10
3 This is confirmed by the following book, which is considered the best spiritual theological study of Saint Irenaeus's teachings. We recommend those who know French to read it: Ysabel de Andia, HOMO VIVENS, Incorruptibility and Divinization of Man according to Irenaeus of Lyon, Paris, 1986, p.59, n.39. The author cites passages from the writings of Father Matthew the Poor in the footnotes of this book (p. 227, footnote number 10 and 11).

is that Christ has encapsulated the entirety of creation and all of history in his blessed person.

The Greek term ἀνακεφαλαιώσασθαι consists of ἀνα-, which implies renewal or ascension, and the verb κεφαλαιόω, derived from κεφάλαιον,[4] which in turn comes from κεφαλή, meaning "head." Thus, the term signifies the renewal and gathering of all things under one head, which is Christ.

It is well-known that Saint Irenaeus wrote in Greek, but his writings reached us in a Latin translation because most of the Greek text is lost, with only a few fragments remaining[5]. The Latin equivalent of this term is Recapitulatio, conveying the same previous meaning, where re- indicates repetition and renewal, and capitula, meaning "heading," is derived from caput, which means "head."

This term is rarely used and only appears twice in the New Testament: in the current verse and in Romans 13:9: "For the commandments, "You shall not commit adultery," "You shall not murder," "You shall not steal," "You shall not bear false witness," "You shall not covet," and if there is any other commandment, are all summed up in this saying, namely, "You shall love your neighbour as yourself.""[6] Here, the term "summed up" implies that this multitude of commandments is included in this single commandment. Thus, the term signifies the gathering of the many into the one that encapsulates everything within itself.

To fully comprehend this verse (Ephesians 1:10), it is essential to consider it in the context in which it was given: It was included in the opening hymn of Apostle Paul's epistle to the Ephesians. He starts the letter with a blessing in verse 3 and continues with a single long spiritual sentence, uninterrupted until verse

---

4 "κεφάλαιον" translates to "topic head", "chapter", or "verse". It is used at the beginning of the Friday Psalmody with the meaning of "important subject": "Indeed, I am approaching a great subject eouni; nkevaleon. "
5 This terminology has been directly adopted from Latin into its derivative languages, such as English and French.
6 Romans 13:9

14, interlaced with the phrase "to the praise of his glory" three times. It could be considered an example of the blessing prayer that the congregation leader would pronounce during the breaking of bread (the Eucharist) in the apostolic church, as the Eucharist was essentially the sacrament of "blessing"[7]: "The cup of blessing which we bless, is it not the communion of the blood of Christ?"[8] Pronouncing the blessing on the bread and wine was the most important act in this sacrament.

The preceding verses in this hymn reveal God's eternal intention for us. He loved us in Christ before all ages and chose us in Him before we existed because He foresaw our complete image in Jesus Christ. God saw mankind at its highest state of perfection in His Son Jesus Christ, who was to be incarnated. He loved humanity in Him and hence chose to create it. Because Christ exists eternally in the bosom and the heart of the Father, and because Christ, due to His forthcoming incarnation, known since eternity to God, represented humanity before the Father, all humanity had a pre-existent existence in the heart of God and in His foreknowledge.

It's clear that this hymn starts by exploring the eternal origins of creation in the heart of God when it was still non-existent, then follows its ascent until it reaches the highest state of existence, which is existence unified with God. This is expressed as uniting all things in Christ, in heaven and on earth.

Creation, united with Jesus Christ, represents the highest level of created existence. We partially experience this now in the mystery of the Church, in the mystery of the divine body. We continue to ascend towards it from glory to glory, as from the Lord, the Spirit. We continue to "grow up in all things into Him who is the head—Christ,"[9] until we arrive "to a perfect man,

---

7 Until the fifth century AD, the Eucharist was referred to in the Church of Alexandria as the "Mystery of the Eulogy", meaning the mystery of blessing, and we see this designation frequently in the writings of St. Cyril the Great.
8 1 Corinthians 10:16
9 Ephesians 4:15

to the measure of the stature of the fullness of Christ"[10]. This mature man in Jesus Christ is the completion of humanity, and indeed of all creation. It is the ascension of creation to the highest state of created existence, which is the ultimate purpose of its creation.

In Romans 8:19, it says: "For the earnest expectation of the creation eagerly waits for the revealing of the sons of God"[11], where "the revealing of the sons of God" signifies humanity reaching the state of adoption in Jesus Christ. We can only achieve this by entering into the only Son, so as to participate - to the extent allowed to us - in His sonship relationship with the Father. The creation's expectation anticipates humanity's entrance into the only Son, that is, the revelation of Christ as the "complete man" who embodies all the redeemed. The creation has been groaning and in labour since its fall with Adam, when "the creation was subjected to futility"[12], and it longs for adoption, which is the entrance of humanity into the only Son. This is the last and final stage of human existence. The first stage was our predestined choice in Jesus Christ before the foundation of the world, and the last stage is for everything to be brought together under one head in Christ, which is the pinnacle of spiritual blessings given to us in Jesus Christ. Due to its importance, Apostle Paul describes it with several theological phrases, namely:

1) The mystery of God

2) The will of God

3) The pleasure of God

4) The eternal purpose of God

5) The administration of the fullness of times.

---

10 Ephesians 4:13
11 Romans 8:19
12 Romans 8:20

To Unite all Things in Christ

All these point to one thing, that is "to bring all things in Christ together".

Thus, the verse states: "having made known to us the mystery of His will, according to His good pleasure which He purposed in Himself, that in the dispensation of the fullness of the times He might gather together in one all things in Christ."[13]

THE MYSTERY OF GOD

The word "mystery" μυστήριον appears frequently in the Letter to the Ephesians[14] . Anyone reading this letter will see how much Saint Paul knew about this mystery:

"By revelation He made known to me the mystery (as I have briefly written already, by which, when you read, you may understand my knowledge in the mystery of Christ)."[15]

The content of "the mystery of Christ" in all the verses that mention it is the union of humanity with God. In the verse we are explaining (1:10), the mystery is defined as " that in the dispensation of the fullness of the times He might gather together in one all things in Christ, both which are in heaven and which are on earth—in Him."[16]

In the third chapter, it is defined as: "that the Gentiles should be fellow heirs, of the same body, and partakers of His promise in Christ through the gospel."[17] So, the mystery of Christ is to make us all partners in His divine body.

In the fifth chapter, after speaking about the mystery of marriage, saying, "the two shall become one flesh"[18] , he adds: "This is a

---

13 Ephesians 1:9-10
14 The word "mystery" = μυστήριον is found in Ephesians 1:9, 3:3-4, 3:9, 5:32, and 6:19.
15 Ephesians 3:3-4
16 Ephesians 1:10
17 Ephesians 3:6
18 Ephesians 5:31

great mystery, but I speak concerning Christ and the church"[19], and explains this by saying: "For we are members of His body, of His flesh and of His bones."[20] Thus, in all these places, the "mystery of Christ" is seen to mean the union of everyone in the divine body.

Then, the Apostle explains that this mystery is the main subject of his preaching:

"To me, who am less than the least of all the saints, this grace was given, that I should preach among the Gentiles the unsearchable riches of Christ, and to make all see what is the fellowship of the mystery, which from the beginning of the ages has been hidden in God who created all things through Jesus Christ." [21]

He had already explained that the content of the mystery is that all nations become partners in one body (3:6), and that Christ gathers us all in His blessed person (1:10). But here he says what he is most interested in is to let us know how we can partake in this mystery, how we can become members of the divine body, of His flesh, and of His bones: "and to make all see what is the fellowship of the mystery"[22].

As for his saying that this mystery was "hidden in God who created all things through Jesus Christ"[23], it means that achieving this mystery (which is "that He might gather together in one all things in Christ") was the ultimate goal hidden in the heart of God before all ages, and for the sake of realising it at the end of ages, God created all that he created. This is the mystery of the creation of the universe; the whole creation was created in the hope of reaching this mystery, in the hope of the peak of creation - which is man - uniting with the Creator in the person of Christ. All creation was created to serve Adam. When the first Adam was created and before he sinned, the animals were

---

19 Ephesians 5:32
20 Ephesians 5:30
21 Ephesians 3:8-9
22 Ibid
23 Ibid

subject to him because they felt that he was the head of all creation, and that he was responsible for achieving the ultimate goal of all creation, which is its union with the Creator Himself in the person of Christ. Therefore, as man approaches his union with Christ, creation submits to him. The spiritual man succeeds in everything, and all creation submits to him and everything he does is successful. Once our spiritual father said that the spiritual man is sensed by the plants and even interacts with them. It is written about Christ: "And He was there in the wilderness forty days, tempted by Satan, and was with the wild beasts"[24], because Christ is the second Adam who renewed and corrected humanity corrupted by the first Adam. Creation originally was subject to the first Adam, but when the first Adam sinned, creation rebelled against him, and the earth began to bring forth thorns and thistles for him, and creation became wild and not subject to him.

When Christ renewed humanity, creation once again became subject to its head, which is man after Christ renewed him. Why? Because it was originally created for him and because he is the one entrusted with achieving the ultimate goal of all creation when he unites with God in the "mystery of Christ": "All are yours…you are Christ's, and Christ is God's."[25]

God's Will

People have many desires, but God has only one constant desire throughout all ages, and that is to glorify His beloved Son, first by creating many through Him ("All things were made through Him, and without Him nothing was made that was made."[26]), then by redeeming them through Him (and thus the Father's glory and the Son's glory are fulfilled - John 13:31 and 17:1), and finally by gathering them all in His body.

---

24 Mark 1:13
25 1 Corinthians 3:22-23
26 John 1:3

That's why Apostle Paul introduces us to the highest form of God's will - "the mystery of His will" - which is to gather everything in Christ: "that in the dispensation of the fullness of the times He might gather together in one all things in Christ, both which are in heaven and which are on earth—in Him."[27] In this sense, we should understand the requests that the Lord taught us to ask: "Your will be done on earth as it is in heaven"[28], meaning let your will be for the salvation of everyone, the return of everyone to you, and finally to gather everyone in Christ, both in heaven and on earth.

Lord Jesus revealed that this is God's constant will throughout the ages, when He stood before Jerusalem and wept over it saying: "O Jerusalem, Jerusalem, the one who kills the prophets and stones those who are sent to her! How often I wanted to gather your children together, as a hen gathers her chicks under her wings, but you were not willing!"[29] Here Christ is speaking as the God of ages who dealt with the people of Israel over hundreds or even thousands of years! How often! How often! How often God wanted to gather His people under His wings, but they were not willing! The entire Old Testament should be read in the light of these words. How many times He told them: "Return, you backsliding children, and I will heal your backslidings"[30], but they "refused to return"[31]. On a wider scale, Jerusalem is a metaphor for all humanity, called to be gathered under the wings of God, indeed, to be gathered in Him in Christ. This is God's constant will throughout the ages: "That in the dispensation of the fullness of the times He might gather together in one all things in Christ".[32] This is the divine will that Lord Jesus prayed for its realisation, earnestly and repetitively, on His last night on earth: "That they all may be one, as You,

---

27 Ephesians 1:10
28 Matthew 6:10
29 Matthew 23:37
30 Jeremiah 3:22
31 Jeremiah 5:3
32 Ephesians 1:10

Father, are in Me, and I in You"[33], and even died to fulfill it, for He died to "gather together in one the children of God who were scattered abroad."[34]

God's Pleasure

It's written in the song of the suffering servant in the Book of Isaiah: "Yet it pleased the Lord to bruise Him; He has put Him to grief."[35] If we search in the prophets for the content of this pleasure, we read in the Book of Ezekiel: "'As I live,' says the Lord God, 'I have no pleasure in the death of the wicked, but that the wicked turn from his way and live."[36]

As for Apostle Paul, he elevates the concept of God's pleasure to a very high level. It's not just about the repentance of the sinner to return and live, but it's about the union of all with Christ: "that in the dispensation of the fullness of the times He might gather together in one all things in Christ, both which are in heaven and which are on earth—in Him."[37]

In this lofty sense, we should understand the voice of the Father that came upon Christ during His baptism and during the Transfiguration: "This is My beloved Son, in whom I am well pleased"[38]. It means the one who fulfills My pleasure, which is that everything will be gathered in Christ, both in heaven and on earth.

God's Intention

The word "intention" is important to the Apostle Paul. In Greek, it is πρόθεσις, composed of two parts: προ- meaning "before," "previous," and θέσις meaning "intention," "theory,"

33 John 17:21
34 John 11:52
35 Isaiah 53:10
36 Ezekiel 33:11
37 Ephesians 1:10
38 Matthew 3:17 and 17:5

"plan"[39]. It comes from the verb τίθημι, which means "to put." So, πρόθεσις means a "previously set intention" or a plan made in advance in God's knowledge, before He began creating the universe. In other words, it's the final vision of creation hidden in God's heart, which He began to actualize when He started creating the entire world, which is "to gather everything in Christ."

This means that before God created the universe, His ultimate intention for creation was clear: to actualize in the end the image of Christ "the fullness of Him who fills all in all."[40] He aimed to gather all the redeemed into His divine body, to gather everything in Christ[41], and thereby realise the image of "the perfect man" (Ephesians 4:13), meaning humanity that has reached the highest level of perfection by uniting with God in Jesus Christ. This is the meaning of "intention" to the Apostle Paul, and he mentions it twice in the first chapter and once in the third chapter of the letter to the Ephesians:

1) "According to His good pleasure, which He purposed[42] in Himself… that He might gather together in one all things in Christ"[43]

2) "In Him also we have obtained an inheritance, being predestined according to the purpose of Him who works all things according to the counsel of His will"[44]

3) "According to the eternal purpose which He accomplished in Christ Jesus our Lord"[45]

---

39 The word "thesis" now means "scientific theory" in English, and its common meaning has become a dissertation or research paper submitted to obtain an academic degree.
40 Ephesians 1:23
41 Ephesians 1:10
42 Here, the word "purpose" is presented in the form of the verb "which He purposed" (ἣν προέθετο), which is from the verb προτίθημι
43 Ephesians 1:9-10
44 Ephesians 1:11
45 Ephesians 3:11

To Unite all Things in Christ
THE ADMINISTRATION OF THE FULFILLMENT OF THE TIMES

We say the word "administration" several times a day in worship. It's "oikonomia"[46] in Greek, and it refers to the administration of the incarnation that ends with the gathering of everything in Christ.

The phrase "the administration of the fullness of the times" has an eschatological character. It suggests to us that at the end of times, God will perform a great work to gather everything in Christ, both things in heaven and things on earth. Like other eschatological matters, this truth is partially experienced now through the Spirit, but its full realization occurs at the end of time or "the fullness of the times."

It should be noted that although eschatological matters can be terrifying to the people of the world—to the point where the Lord said, "men's hearts failing them from fear and the expectation of those things which are coming on the earth,"[47] —for believers, these are positive matters containing a greater grace. Hence, the Lord followed up by saying to the believers, "when these things begin to happen, look up and lift up your heads, because your redemption draws near."[48] That's why the early Christians eagerly awaited these eschatological events, their favourite cry being "come, Lord Jesus!" (1 Corinthians 16:22; Revelation 22:20). This is because they were certain that His coming would be accompanied by extraordinary grace[49], as Saint Peter said:

---

46 In Greek, it's οἰκονομία, which literally means: a system or arrangement of a house (from οἶκος = house, and νόμος = law or arrangement). So, the word originally means the management or organization of household affairs or the like. But its theological meaning is defined as the provision of the incarnation and redemption, which, as the verse says, ends with "gathering everything in Christ".
47 Luke 21:26
48 Luke 21:28
49 The Didache (which is contemporary with the time of writing the Gospel of John) tells us that at the end of the Eucharist, they used to shout together: Let grace come and let this world pass away! (Didache 10:6)

"Therefore gird up the loins of your mind, be sober, and rest your hope fully upon the grace that is to be brought to you at the revelation of Jesus Christ."[50]

The same Saint Peter used eschatological phrases with a profoundly positive meaning in his speech in the book of Acts:

"Repent therefore and be converted, that your sins may be blotted out, so that times of refreshing may come from the presence of the Lord, and that He may send Jesus Christ, who was preached to you before, whom heaven must receive until the times of restoration of all things, which God has spoken by the mouth of all His holy prophets since the world began."[51]

In this statement, note two expressions with very positive eschatological meanings: "times of refreshing" and "times of restoration of all things."

Their purpose in light of the verse we are explaining: the times of refreshing and the times of restoration of all things are when the "administration of the fullness of the times" takes place, which is to "gather together in one all things in Christ, both which are in heaven and which are on earth—in Him."[52]

This is the meaning of the phrase "restoration of all things," which is the return of everything to its original state. Because Adam, before he sinned, was unified in the sight of God. But after he sinned, humanity was struck by the disease of division, first evident when Cain killed his brother Abel. Therefore, many

---

50 1 Peter 1:13
51 Acts 3:19-21
52 Ephesians 1:10

Fathers consider that the division of humanity came as a direct result of Adam's fall and fragmentation due to sin[53]:

"Adam fell and thus seemed to shatter, scattering his fragments all over the world."[54]

"Due to sin, the singular human nature was torn into a thousand pieces!"[55]

That's why the Lord came:

"To set right mankind and gather again its scattered members." [56]

"To restore life to mankind, and gather its members that were dispersed by death, because death had divided man." [57]

The clearest manifestation of the fragmentation of humanity and the dispersion of its members was the division of nations that occurred with the confusion of tongues at the Tower of Babel.

Christ came to heal humanity's sickness caused by sin and "restore all things to their origin," meaning to justify Adam from sin and return him to his original unity before God. Christ even elevated this unity immeasurably, making it not a unity for humanity in itself, as it was in Adam, but a unity for humanity in

---

53 Father Matthew the Poor says: "Due to sin, humanity has fragmented into multiple, even shattered, divided bodies. This division has no limit, humanity surpasses continual division in every field and in every entity, nation against nation, church against church, family against family, father against son, spouse against spouse, and the soul, in the depth of its single entity, is divided against itself! This internal division that overflows onto every form and appearance is the general disease of humanity, it begins with the single soul and ends with all humanity. And sin is this disease itself, it is the features of all its symptoms, causes, and results!!" (Article "The Heavens Were Split" in the book Feasts of Divine Manifestation).
54 Saint Augustine, in his commentary on Psalms 95: 1 PL 37, 1236
55 Maximus the Confessor PG 90,
56 Pope Alexandros of Alexandria, Sermon on the Soul, the Body and the Pains of the Lord ANF VI, 302
57 Saint Meliton, Bishop of Sardis (passed away around AD 180) SC 123, 238

IN HIM

God: "That they may be one in us," "gather together in one all things in Christ."⁵⁸

The first visible realiSation of this unity was what happened on Pentecost, when people of various nations and different languages gathered in Jerusalem and all merged into one body by the action of the Holy Spirit. Luke, the author of Acts, intentionally mentions in the narrative of this story the names of various nations and peoples with different languages who all gathered in Jerusalem on that day: "Parthians and Medes and Elamites, those dwelling in Mesopotamia, Judea and Cappadocia, Pontus and Asia, Phrygia and Pamphylia, Egypt and the parts of Libya adjoining Cyrene, visitors from Rome, both Jews and proselytes, Cretans and Arabs"⁵⁹. More than fourteen nations of people all joined the one body of Christ on that day by the action of the Holy Spirit: "For by one Spirit we were all baptized into one body—whether Jews or Greeks, whether slaves or free—and have all been made to drink into one Spirit."⁶⁰

Therefore, many Fathers consider that what happened on Pentecost was the direct opposite of the scattering of the nations that happened at the Tower of Babel. For example, St. Cyril the Great says:

"The multiplicity of tongues at the Tower of Babel was a sign of division and scattering among all nations. In Christ, however, speaking in tongues on Pentecost became a sign of gathering in the unity of the Spirit." ⁶¹

He shares the comparison between the division that occurred at the Tower of Babel and the unity of nations that occurred on Pentecost with Saints John Chrysostom ⁶², Gregory of Nazianzus⁶³, and Cyril of Jerusalem ⁶⁴.

58 Ephesians 1:10
59 Acts 2: 9-11
60 1 Corinthians 12: 13
61 Glossary on the Book of Genesis PG 69, 80
62 Sermon on Pentecost Day PG 50, 467
63 Sermon 41 on Pentecost: 16.
64 Sermon 17: 7

To Unite all Things in Christ

Thus, what happened on Pentecost was the beginning of restoring humanity to its original unity that it had before the fall, the beginning of what will happen in the "times of refreshing" and the "times of restoration of all things," which is: "to gather all things in Christ!"

"TO GATHER TOGETHER IN ONE ALL THINGS IN CHRIST."

This is the desire of God throughout all ages, indeed, His desire before all ages. It is the "eternal purpose" hidden in the heart of God from eternity, and for its realisation at the end of ages, in the "fullness of times," God began to create the whole universe, gradually guiding it, little by little, through discipline, cultivation, and redemption, until He brings it at the end of ages to this blissful conclusion.

This is the climax of Christ's glory. If Christ was first glorified by creating many in Him, "All things were made through Him, and without Him nothing was made that was made"[65]; then He was glorified even more by their redemption through Him - as appears in the Gospel of John that the glory of Christ and the Father is manifested in the redemption of mankind (John 13:31 and 17:1) – the pinnacle of Christ's glory comes when "He might gather together in one all things in Christ, both which are in heaven and which are on earth—in Him."[66]

This is the steadfast will of God throughout all ages, which He never ceased trying to fulfill in every generation, as it appears from Christ's words to Jerusalem, in His capacity as the God of Israel, who dealt with it over hundreds, indeed thousands of years: " "O Jerusalem, Jerusalem, the one who kills the prophets and stones those who are sent to her! How often I wanted to

---
65 John 1:3
66 Ephesians 1:10

gather your children together, as a hen gathers her chicks under her wings, but you were not willing!"[67]

This statement by the Lord: "how often!" a cry of sadness that wrenches our hearts, invites us to reread the entire Old Testament in its light, to sense this unchanging divine will throughout the ages, which the Lord has long desired to achieve, but they were not willing. How often the Lord said to them: if you listen to my words and obey me, even if you were scattered to the ends of the sky, from there I will gather you to me!

Saint Peter speaks of "times of restoration of all things" that "God has spoken by the mouth of all His holy prophets since the world began"[68]. Indeed, the books of the prophets are full of God's promises about times when the Lord will turn away ungodliness from His people (Romans 11:26) and gather His people back to Him. Although they mostly come in a material, earthly style – so that people at that time could comprehend them – they deserve to be presented here, because they reflect to us the longing of God's heart throughout all ages. They are considered, in the language of the book of Hebrews, a "shadow" (8:5) of the great truth that filled God's heart and which He intended to achieve at the end of ages when the time for the "dispensation of the fulness of times" comes, and "He might gather together in one all things in Christ, both which are in heaven and which are on earth—in Him"[69].

Here are the divine promises in the Old Testament about God gathering His people to Him,

Deuteronomy 30:1-4: "Now it shall come to pass, when all these things come upon you, the blessing and the curse which I have set before you, and you call them to mind among all the nations where the Lord your God drives you, and you return to the Lord your God and obey His voice, according to all that I command you today, you and your children, with all your heart and with

---

67 Matthew 23:37
68 Acts 3:21
69 Ephesians 1:10

all your soul, that the Lord your God will bring you back from captivity, and have compassion on you, and gather you again from all the nations where the Lord your God has scattered you. If any of you are driven out to the farthest parts under heaven, from there the Lord your God will gather you, and from there He will bring you."

Nehemiah 1:8-9: "Remember, I pray, the word that You commanded Your servant Moses, saying, 'If you are unfaithful, I will scatter you among the nations; but if you return to Me, and keep My commandments and do them, though some of you were cast out to the farthest part of the heavens, yet I will gather them from there, and bring them to the place which I have chosen as a dwelling for My name.'"

Psalms 147:2: "The Lord builds up Jerusalem; He gathers together the outcasts of Israel."

Isaiah 11:12-13: "He will set up a banner for the nations, and will assemble the outcasts of Israel, and gather together the dispersed of Judah from the four corners of the earth. Also the envy of Ephraim shall depart, and the adversaries of Judah shall be cut off; Ephraim shall not envy Judah, And Judah shall not harass Ephraim."

Isaiah 40:11: "He will feed His flock like a shepherd; He will gather the lambs with His arm, and carry them in His bosom, and gently lead those who are with young."

Isaiah 43:5-6: "Fear not, for I am with you; I will bring your descendants from the east, and gather you from the west; I will say to the north, 'Give them up!' and to the south, 'Do not keep them back!' Bring My sons from afar, and My daughters from the ends of the earth."

Isaiah 49:5-6, 11-12, 18: "And now the LORD says, Who formed Me from the womb to be His Servant, to bring Jacob back to Him, so that Israel is gathered to Him...Indeed He says, 'It is too small a thing that You should be My Servant to raise up the tribes of Jacob, and to restore the preserved ones of Israel; I will also give You as a light to the Gentiles, that You should be My salvation to the ends of the earth.'...I will make each of My mountains a road, and My highways shall be elevated. Surely these shall come from afar; Look! Those from the north and the west, and these from the land of Sinim...Lift up your eyes, look around and see; all these gather together and come to you. As I live," says the LORD, "You shall surely clothe yourselves with them all as an ornament, and bind them on you as a bride does."

Isaiah 54:7: "For a mere moment I have forsaken you, but with great mercies I will gather you."

Isaiah 56:7-8: "Even them I will bring to My holy mountain, and make them joyful in My house of prayer. Their burnt offerings and their sacrifices will be accepted on My altar; For My house shall be called a house of prayer for all nations. The Lord GOD, who gathers the outcasts of Israel, says, 'Yet I will gather to him others besides those who are gathered to him.'"

Isaiah 60:1, 2, 3, 4, 22: "Arise, shine; For your light has come! And the glory of the LORD is risen upon you. For behold, the darkness shall cover the earth, and deep darkness the people; but the LORD will arise over you, and His glory will be seen upon you. The Gentiles shall come to your light, and kings to the brightness of your rising. Lift up your eyes all around, and see: they all gather together, they come to you; your sons shall come from afar, and your daughters shall be nursed at your side...I, the LORD, will hasten it in its time."

Isaiah 66:8: "Who has heard such a thing? Who has seen such things? Shall the earth be made to give birth in one day? Or shall a nation be born at once? For as soon as Zion was in labor, She gave birth to her children."

Isaiah 66:18: "For I know their works and their thoughts. It shall be that I will gather all nations and tongues; and they shall come and see My glory."

Isaiah 66:20: "Then they shall bring all your brethren for an offering to the LORD out of all nations, on horses and in chariots and in litters, on mules and on camels, to My holy mountain Jerusalem,' says the LORD, 'as the children of Israel bring an offering in a clean vessel into the house of the LORD."

Isaiah 66:23: "And it shall come to pass that from one New Moon to another, and from one Sabbath to another, all flesh shall come to worship before Me," says the LORD."

Jeremiah 3:17: "At that time Jerusalem shall be called The Throne of the LORD, and all the nations shall be gathered to it, to the name of the LORD, to Jerusalem. No more shall they follow the dictates of their evil hearts."

Jeremiah 3:18: "In those days the house of Judah shall walk with the house of Israel, and they shall come together out of the land of the north to the land that I have given as an inheritance to your fathers."

Jeremiah 23:1: "Woe to the shepherds who destroy and scatter the sheep of My pasture!" says the LORD."

Jeremiah 23:2: "Therefore thus says the LORD God of Israel against the shepherds who feed My people: 'You have scattered My flock, driven them away, and not attended to them. Behold, I will attend to you for the evil of your doings,' says the LORD."

Jeremiah 23:3: "But I will gather the remnant of My flock out of all countries where I have driven them, and bring them back to their folds; and they shall be fruitful and increase."

Jeremiah 29:13: "And you will seek Me and find Me, when you search for Me with all your heart."

Jeremiah 29:14: "I will be found by you, says the LORD, and I will bring you back from your captivity; I will gather you from all the nations and from all the places where I have driven you, says the LORD, and I will bring you to the place from which I cause you to be carried away captive."

Jeremiah 30:3: "For behold, the days are coming,' says the LORD, 'that I will bring back from captivity My people Israel and Judah,' says the LORD. 'And I will cause them to return to the land that I gave to their fathers, and they shall possess it.'"

Jeremiah 31:8: "Behold, I will bring them from the north country, and gather them from the ends of the earth, among them the blind and the lame, the woman with child and the one who labors with child, together; a great throng shall return there."

Jeremiah 31:10: "Hear the word of the LORD, O nations, and declare it in the isles afar off, and say, 'He who scattered Israel will gather him, and keep him as a shepherd does his flock.'"

Jeremiah 32:37: "Behold, I will gather them out of all countries where I have driven them in My anger, in My fury, and in great wrath; I will bring them back to this place, and I will cause them to dwell safely."

Jeremiah 32:38: "They shall be My people, and I will be their God."

Jeremiah 50:4: "In those days and in that time," says the LORD, "The children of Israel shall come, They and the children of Judah together; with continual weeping they shall come, and seek the LORD their God."

Jeremiah 50:5: "They shall ask the way to Zion, with their faces toward it, saying, 'Come and let us join ourselves to the LORD in a perpetual covenant that will not be forgotten.'"

Ezekiel 11:17: "Therefore say, 'Thus says the Lord GOD: "I will gather you from the peoples, assemble you from the countries where you have been scattered, and I will give you the land of Israel."'"

Ezekiel 20:34: "I will bring you out from the peoples and gather you out of the countries where you are scattered, with a mighty hand, with an outstretched arm, and with fury poured out."

Ezekiel 20:40: "For on My holy mountain, on the mountain height of Israel," says the Lord GOD, "there all the house of Israel, all of them in the land, shall serve Me; there I will accept them, and there I will require your offerings and the firstfruits of your sacrifices, together with all your holy things."

Ezekiel 20:41: "I will accept you as a sweet aroma when I bring you out from the peoples and gather you out of the countries where you have been scattered; and I will be hallowed in you before the Gentiles."

Ezekiel 22:19-21: "Therefore thus says the Lord GOD: 'Because you have all become dross, therefore behold, I will gather you into the midst of Jerusalem. As men gather silver, bronze, iron, lead, and tin into the midst of a furnace, to blow the fire on it, to melt it; so I will gather you in My anger and in My fury, and I will leave you there and melt you. Yes, I will gather you and blow on you with the fire of My wrath, and you shall be melted in its midst.'"

Ezekiel 28:25: "Thus says the Lord GOD: 'When I have gathered the house of Israel from the peoples among whom they are scattered, and am hallowed in them in the sight of the Gentiles, then they will dwell in their own land which I gave to My servant Jacob.'"

Ezekiel 34:12,13,15: "As a shepherd seeks out his flock on the day he is among his scattered sheep, so will I seek out My sheep and deliver them from all the places where they were scattered on a cloudy and dark day. And I will bring them out from the peoples and gather them from the countries, and will bring them to their own land; I will feed them on the mountains of Israel, in the valleys and in all the inhabited places of the country... I will feed My flock, and I will make them lie down,' says the Lord GOD."

Ezekiel 36:22,23,24,27,28: "Therefore say to the house of Israel, 'Thus says the Lord GOD: "I do not do this for your sake, O house of Israel, but for My holy name's sake, which you have profaned among the nations wherever you went. And I will sanctify My great name, which has been profaned among the nations, which you have profaned in their midst; and the nations shall know that I am the LORD," says the Lord GOD, "when I am hallowed in you before their eyes. For I will take you from among the nations, gather you out of all countries, and bring you into your own land... I will put My Spirit within you and cause you to walk in My statutes, and you will keep My judgments and do them. Then you shall dwell in the land that I gave to your fathers; you shall be My people, and I will be your God."

Ezekiel 37:21,22: "Then say to them, 'Thus says the Lord GOD: "Surely I will take the children of Israel from among the nations, wherever they have gone, and will gather them from every side and bring them into their own land; and I will make them one nation in the land, on the mountains of Israel; and one king shall be king over them all; they shall no longer be two nations, nor shall they ever be divided into two kingdoms again."

Ezekiel 39:25,27,28: "Therefore thus says the Lord GOD: 'Now I will bring back the captives of Jacob, and have mercy on the whole house of Israel; and I will be jealous for My holy name... When I have brought them back from the peoples and gathered them out of their enemies' lands, and I am hallowed in them in the sight of many nations, then they shall know that I am the LORD their God, who sent them into captivity among the nations, but also brought them back to their land, and left none of them captive any longer."

Hosea 1:11: "Then the children of Judah and the children of Israel Shall be gathered together, And appoint for themselves one head[70]; And they shall come up out of the land, For great will be the day of Jezreel!"

---

[70] This verse is remarkable because it perfectly corresponds to the meaning of the word ἀνακεφαλαιώσασθαι (Ephesians 1:10) which means to gather under one head.

To Unite all Things in Christ

Micah 2:12: "I will surely assemble all of you, O Jacob, I will surely gather the remnant of Israel; I will put them together like sheep of the fold, Like a flock in the midst of their pasture; They shall make a loud noise because of so many people."

Micah 4:6,7: "In that day," says the LORD, "I will assemble the lame, I will gather the outcast And those whom I have afflicted; I will make the lame a remnant, And the outcast a strong nation; So the LORD will reign over them in Mount Zion From now on, even forever."

Zephaniah 3:18-20: "'I will gather those who sorrow over the appointed assembly, Who are among you, To whom its reproach is a burden. Behold, at that time I will deal with all who afflict you; I will save the lame, And gather those who were driven out; I will appoint them for praise and fame In every land where they were put to shame. At that time I will bring you back, Even at the time I gather you; For I will give you fame and praise Among all the peoples of the earth, When I return your captives before your eyes,' Says the LORD."

Zechariah 10:6,8,10: "'I will strengthen the house of Judah, And I will save the house of Joseph. I will bring them back, Because I have mercy on them. They shall be as though I had not cast them aside; For I am the LORD their God, And I will hear them... I will whistle for them and gather them, For I have redeemed them[71] ; And they shall increase as they once increased... I will also bring them back from the land of Egypt, And gather them from Assyria. I will bring them into the land of Gilead and Lebanon, Until no more room is found for them.'"

These extensive collection of prophecies and promises, which came over separated periods of time, starting from the days of Moses to the last of the minor prophets before the divine revelation ceased from Israel, reveals to us God's consistent will throughout the ages in all his dealings with his people, Israel.

---

[71] This verse shows the connection of "bringing everything together" (Ephesians 1:10) with the preceding step, which is redemption: "In him we have redemption through his blood" (Ephesians 1:7).

Furthermore, it uncovers what was brewing in the heart of Christ when he wept over Jerusalem, saying: "How often I wanted...but you would not!"[72]

Even though most of these prophecies were delivered in a contemporary earthly style, like everything in the Old Testament, they pointed beyond that to a greater spiritual truth. This great truth was announced to the Apostle Paul as the mystery of God: "gather together in one all things in Christ."[73] It is the "mystery of Christ" that the Gentiles are partners in the one body, in Christ. This is the "eternal purpose" that was hidden in God's heart before all ages, and for which God created everything to fulfill in the end of time.

Now we understand why the Apostle Paul elevates this truth beyond measure and presents it to us as the mystery of God, the will of God, His pleasure, His purpose, and the culmination of divine arrangement, "He might gather together in one all things in Christ, both which are in heaven and which are on earth—in Him."[74]

"WHICH ARE IN HEAVEN AND WHICH ARE ON EART."

This part of the verse shows that the angels and all the heavenly forces have a share in the collective gathering under one head in Christ. However, their position in Christ differs from ours because Christ did not unite with the nature of angels, but He united with our human nature: "For indeed He does not give aid to angels, but He does give aid to the seed of Abraham ."[75]

---

72 Matthew 23:37
73 Ephesians 1:10
74 Ibid
75 Hebrews 2:16

" [76]Hence, because of His incarnation in our nature, we have received things "which angels desire to look into"[77] and we have the privilege to tell them about it:

"that now the manifold wisdom of God might be made known by the church to the principalities and powers in the heavenly places,"[78].

Here the "manifold" wisdom of God refers to God's creation of the heavenly ranks, with their superhuman spiritual natures, far beyond what we know. Then the "manifold wisdom of God" started to create the physical world with everything in it, and at its pinnacle, God created man, an intelligent being with a nature much weaker than the angels' nature, because it is tied to the matter taken from the dust of the earth. However, God greatly empathised with man because of his weakness. So, when man fell, God sent His Son to unite with human nature, and this weak nature received an immense grace and limitless dignity because of God's Son's union with it. This is God's manifold wisdom that gave the weakest higher dignity and greater grace.

Here, Apostle Paul envisages the redeemed humanity in blissful eternity, telling the hosts of angels about the grace that called her from darkness into His marvellous light, who redeemed her with His blood, and who made her partaker of the divine nature. Humanity has received what the angels cannot reach, as we say in our praise:

They surround you: Cherubim and Seraphim: they can't even look at you. And we behold you every day: on the altar: and partake of your Body and precious Blood.

God has gathered us with the angels under one head in Christ. And here we are, telling them what God has done for us: "I will

---

76 It means that he united with the body taken from the Virgin, who is a descendant of Abraham, in order to fulfill the promise given to Abraham: "In your offspring, all nations of the earth will be blessed" (Genesis 22:18).
77 1 Peter 1:12
78 Ephesians 3:10

IN HIM

sing to you before the angels"[79], so they too might increase in offering the "praise of victory and salvation that is ours," with ceaseless voices and much greater enthusiasm than we can offer, because they have superior abilities to praise. We need them because they fulfill on our behalf the superior debt of praise and thanksgiving that we should offer to God for the great things He has given us. And they benefit from the superior grace given to us as it gives them a greater chance to increase their gratitude and praise to God with more enthusiasm. And in this way, God was able to make all His creation happy with His "manifold wisdom".

Sayings of Saint Irenaeus on the Gathering of All Things in Christ:

Christ encapsulated all the history that preceded him in His blessed person:

"That's why Saint Luke presents a lineage of Christ that starts from the birth of our Lord to Adam, covering 72 generations, thus connecting the end with the beginning, and implying that the Lord is the one who gathered recapitulatus = ἀνακεφαλαιωσάμενος (or encapsulated) in Himself all the nations that branched out from Adam, and all tongues of people and their generations, including Adam himself"[80]

Here, Saint Irenaeus explains how the nations of the earth branched out from the first Adam, and how when Christ (the second Adam) was born from all these lineages, He seems to have gathered in Himself again all the peoples, including Adam himself. The first Adam is the origin of branching out, and the last Adam is the principle of gathering and returning to unity.

"Indeed, when He incarnated and became human, He gathered recapitulauit = ἀνεκεφαλαιώσατο (or encapsulated) in Himself the long human history and granted us salvation concentrated in

---
79 Psalm 137:1 in the Septuagint and in the Coptic translation.
80 Against Heresies 3: 22: 3 AH III,22,3

Himself, so that what we lost in Adam, being in the image and likeness of God, we regain it in Christ Jesus"[81]

Christ gathered in Himself the long human history... He encapsulated in Himself all human misery and sorrow, starting from Adam's cry when leaving paradise, passing by Jeremiah's laments and his crying over Jerusalem[82]. He took all our sorrow into Himself and turned it into joy, He took all our negatives and turned them into positives, He took our illnesses and turned them into healing, He took our destruction and turned it into salvation.

"THE GOAL OF INCARNATION CHRIST GATHERING EVERYTHING IN HIMSELF"

"There is one God, who is God the Father, and one Christ who is our Lord Jesus Christ, who came fulfilling all providence and gathering recapitulans= ἀνακεφαλαιωσάμενος (or summarizing) in Himself all things, including man, who is the creation of God. He gathered recapitulatus = ἀνεκεφαλαιώσατο man also to Himself. What was invisible became visible, what was not understood became understood, what was not suffering became suffering, and the Word became flesh, thus gathering recapitulans = ἀνακεφαλαιωσάμενος everything in Himself, so just as the Word of God is the first among the heavenly and spiritual beings that are invisible, He also becomes the first among the visible and physical beings. By taking this priority, He becomes the head of the church (Eph 1:22), to draw everything to Himself (John 12:32)[83]."

---

81 Against Heresies 3: 18: 1 AH III,18,1
82 Therefore, the Lamentations of Jeremiah, which begin with "I am the man," are read and attributed to the mouth of Christ on Good Friday.
83 Against Heresies 3: 16: 6 AH III,16,6

IN HIM

Here is a reference to Christ's saying, "And I, if I am lifted up from the earth, will draw all peoples to Myself"[84]. Saint Irenaeus believes that this is the purpose of Christ's incarnation: to gather everyone in Himself and draw everyone to Him.

"Gathering everything in Christ" is not only the goal of the incarnation, but also the goal of the cross:

"The Word, which was inscribed on all creation in the form of a cross, and which ruled and directed all things, came to His own in a visible way, became flesh, and was hung on a piece of wood, so that all things might be gathered recapituletur = ἀνακεφαλαιώσηται in Himself"[85]

Here it is considered that "gathering everything in Christ" is not only the goal of the incarnation but is also the goal of the cross. Paul the Apostle preceded him in this, saying that Christ "and that He might reconcile them both to God in one body through the cross, thereby putting to death the enmity."[86]

Saint Irenaeus refers to this verse: "One of our predecessors (referring to Apostle Paul) said, 'When He spread out His divine arms, He gathered the two nations together into one God.' There were two arms due to the existence of two separate nations to the ends of the earth, but there was one head in the middle due to the existence of one God who is over all, through all, and in all of us"[87].

Christ's work in His second coming: gathering everything in Himself

---

84 John 12:32
85 Against Heresies 5: 18: 3 AH V,18,3
86 Ephesians 2:16
87 Against Heresies 5: 17: 4 AH V,17,4 In the same context, Saint Athanasius says: If by his death he abolished the middle wall of partition (Eph 2:14), and the call went out to all nations, how could he call us if he had not been crucified? For only on the cross does a man die with his hands outstretched. Therefore, it was fitting for the Lord to bear this and stretch out his hands so that with one hand he could draw the ancient people and with the other the nations, and unify the two in himself (On the Incarnation of the Word 25:3).

To Unite all Things in Christ

An early version of the law of faith: Here Saint Irenaeus presents a concise version of the law of faith. Noting that he wrote more than a hundred years before the Council of Nicaea, and on the other hand, he was a direct disciple of Polycarp who saw the apostles and was a disciple of them. Therefore, we should believe him when he tells us that what he is saying is a transmission from the apostles themselves:

"The church, although spread throughout the inhabited earth from one end to the other, received from the apostles and their disciples a single faith in one God, the Father, the Ruler of all, Creator of the heaven, the earth, the sea, and everything in them, and in Christ Jesus, the only Son of God, who for our salvation incarnated from the Holy Spirit, who declared through the prophets the arrangement of the coming of our beloved Lord Jesus Christ, His virgin birth, His sufferings, His resurrection from the dead, His bodily ascension to the heavens, His second coming from the heavens in the glory of the Father, to gather everything in Himself ἐπὶ τὸ ἀνακεφαλαιώσασθαι τὰ πάντα ἐν αὐτῷ, and to raise the entire body of humanity and restore it to life, so that every knee in heaven and on earth bows before our Lord and our God and our Savior and our King Jesus Christ, according to the will of the unseen Father[88]."

In this summarised form of faith, it is noted that Saint Irenaeus includes the dear doctrine to him, that Christ in His second coming will gather everything in Himself, according to what is mentioned in Ephesians 1:10.

Finally, total gathering will take place in the Father's embrace. "For righteousness alone, He gave Himself for us, to gather us all in the Father's embrace!" [89]

---

[88] Against Heresies 1: 10: 1-2 AH I,10,1-2
[89] Against Heresies 5: 2: 1 AH V,2,1

www.ingramcontent.com/pod-product-compliance
Lightning Source LLC
Chambersburg PA
CBHW031643170426
43195CB00035B/565